Answering the C... .. ..

"Elemental beings did not exist for me prior to reading this book. I could conceive of the possibility of their existence and that clairvoyant people could perceive them. (How else did they get into all those fairy tales?) I could imagine that a person with supersensitive abilities might meet gnomes and elves in the forest but that such an unbelievable wealth and diversity of ensouled beings exist inside and around us, this is truly overwhelming."

—**Christiane Flocken,** M.D. (alternative medicine)
and psychotherapist

"Answering the Call of the Elementals touched me deeply. Besides its message, I greatly appreciate the openness and precision with which the author describes his spiritual experiences."

—**Helmut Thomas,** Waldorf teacher

"It is a little miracle how Thomas Mayer manages to assuage my critical mind right from the beginning of the book. I was drawn into a story that is entertaining and gives incredible joy. This little miracle is possible because Thomas Mayer presents himself purely as himself. His sentences are not overly complex, they are precise, without pretense, and full of flashes of humor not explicitly intended."

—**Enno Schmidt,** artist, writer, and civil rights activist
engaged in the Basic Income Earth Network (BIEN)

"I devoured *Answering the Call of the Elementals*. I was deeply moved by Mayer's work, his authenticity, and the matter-of-fact way with which he gives us so much important information in the finest and clearest way. This book contains so many treasures to take away."

—**Seraina Seyffer,** therapist

"This book is fantastic! I just finished reading it and have already gifted it to three people. It is wonderfully written with descriptions of how to come into contact with and perceive the elementals. Again and again I noticed while reading how I was totally filled with warmth, light, and strength. Moreover, I have for the first time understood the necessity of caring for the elementals, because in the end it is synonymous with caring for the earth and its beings."

—**Claudine Nierth,**
spokesperson for the board for More Democracy

Answering the Call of the Elementals

Practices for Connecting with Nature Spirits

Thomas Mayer

Translated by Agnes Hardorp

FINDHORN PRESS

Findhorn Press
One Park Street
Rochester, Vermont 05767
www.findhornpress.com

Findhorn Press is a division of Inner Traditions International

Originally published in German in 2008 by Neue Erde
Verlag GmbH under the title *Rettet die Elementarwesen.*
Published in English in 2021 by Findhorn Press.

Disclaimer
The information in this book is given in good faith and intended for
information only. Neither author nor publisher can be held liable by
any person for any loss or damage whatsoever which may arise from the
use of this book or any of the information therein.

Cataloging-in-Publication data for this title
is available from the Library of Congress

ISBN 978-1-64411-214-4 (print)
ISBN 978-1-64411-215-1 (ebook)

Printed and bound in the United States by Versa Press, Inc.

10 9 8 7 6 5 4 3 2 1

Edited by Nicky Leach
Text design and layout by Anna-Kristina Larsson
This book was typeset in Garamond and Metropolis

To send correspondence to the author of this book,
mail a first-class letter to the author c/o Inner Traditions •
Bear & Company, One Park Street, Rochester, VT 05767, USA
and we will forward the communication, or contact
the author directly at **www.thomasmayer.org**.

Contents

Introduction

Even if we are not consciously aware of it, we live in the realm of elemental beings. Everywhere, and all the time, they penetrate our souls and slip into our hearts. The whole world around us is ensouled with elemental beings. Elemental beings participate in everything that is happening in nature around us.

Our inner world, the world of our thoughts and feelings, is made of elementals. And we constantly produce new ones. In almost all walks of life we are dealing with elemental beings. The elemental beings are nearer to us than we think!

This book is concerned with all the realms of elemental beings I know about. I have tried to be as comprehensible and authentic as possible. A personal rendering seemed most appropriate for this. I did not want to write an abstract book but, rather, to invite you to participate in my experience.

There is no abstract or general experience of elemental beings; there are only ever specific human beings who connect to specific elemental beings. They carry these elemental beings around with them as part of their constitution. This is why I always describe the specific circumstances, and as precisely as possible, my ways and methods of experiencing our elemental friends.

My descriptions are of course very limited. I only know a few elementals in a deeper way. That is why, in one of the chapters, I discuss books about elemental beings by people who have written out of direct experience. I owe a lot to these authors, who have enhanced my own experience in numerous ways.

I have been interested in gaining a direct experience of the spiritual world since I was a young man. I studied a great deal of spiritual literature and took up the anthroposophical meditative path of schooling formulated by Rudolf Steiner, but made no progress in my ability to perceive elemental beings.

I received practical help in developing my faculties in 2003, through a series of workshops on geomancy, a study of the super-sensible level of landscapes, gardens, and habitats. Since then, I have been able to regularly connect consciously with elemental beings. Based on my own experiences, I believe that a great unearthed treasure of possibilities of perceiving elemental beings is hidden in human beings. This was not the case 20 years ago, but our possibilities for conscious perception have advanced since then.

Every year, I lead approximately 30 meditation courses, which all include a short introduction to perceiving elemental beings. Every time, I am surprised by how well this works after an appropriate meditative preparation. The participants have pretty evident experiences that mutually reinforce each other; therefore, I know not just that the elemental beings are much closer to us than we believe but we also have many more possibilities of perceiving them than we think. However, these possibilities can only unfold if developed, and if clear and practical concepts of elemental beings and clear methods for perception are presented.

This is why I began writing. *Answering the Call of the Elementals* is the first book in a series. It is a personal introduction to the world of elemental beings, with the theme: This is how I do it.

In the second and third books, *Collaboration with Elemental Beings*, I interviewed more than 30 people who perceive elementals. I spoke with them about how they experience them, what they pay particular attention to, how they prepare for this interaction, how this ability developed in them, and what special encounters they have had. Each and every one has an individual approach. We can learn a lot from them. With these two books, I want to make this wealth of experience visible and accessible to all, with the theme: This is how others do it.

In the summer of 2007, we drove to a little fishing village called Valun, on the island of Cres, Croatia, for a vacation. I wanted to start writing about elemental beings, but I had hardly got down to what I had planned to write before the elemental beings of Cres got involved and a momentum of its own developed.

᚛ 1 ᚜
The Plea

It is an unforgettable morning in the fall of 2004. I am in Hamburg with Agnes, my beloved partner, in her penthouse apartment doing our morning meditation.

I need to mention two prior events to make the following comprehensible. First, Agnes and I have just given our first course in anthroposophic meditation at a summer conference in Hibernia (a Waldorf school in the west of Germany) a few months earlier. There was a great deal of interest, it was very uplifting, and we are now considering offering more courses in the future.

Second, I met geomancers Wolfgang Schneider and Fritz Bachmann a year ago, in 2003, and these encounters have had many consequences. After learning how geomancers do it, I have finally found a soul path to experience elemental beings that I can walk on my own. I have received several important keys I had been missing, and now I can sometimes open the door a little and slip into the elemental world with my own consciousness.

This morning, Agnes and I have just completed a word meditation, and I am now trying to stay in pure awareness. This is the state of consciousness before thoughts, feelings, and perceptions occur, a dwelling in a spiritual plane.

I am startled. Something is blowing my way, coming nearer. Before my inner eye, figures form—four schematic figures, more thought than picture. At the same time, I feel like I am expanding all over the world, connected to it by love and responsibility. I find myself no longer in Hamburg but encompassing the whole earth. By this I do not mean the physical earth; I mean the level underlying the earth—the world of the elemental beings. I feel lovingly responsible for the elemental beings of this cosmos. These feelings do not come from me but emanate from these four beings and fill me from the inside. As images in my imagination, they appear quite small and imperceptible. In my experience, though, they are big—profoundly big.

The four figures begin to differentiate, and it becomes clear. One figure feels responsible for the earth beings of our cosmos, another for the water beings, the third for the fire beings, and the fourth for the air and light beings. Then the figures are again superimposed.

I ask, "Who are you?"

The answer is there lightning fast, not as a word but as a wordless thought. I know this from conversations with spiritual beings.

I try to formulate this wordless thought impulse into words.

We are the beings of the nature elementals. We encompass and represent them. We come to you with a request. Humanity has forgotten the elemental beings. We live in your subconscious, we are a big part of your lives, but you know nothing about us. This was necessary. But now the time has come for us elemental beings to lead a conscious life together with you again. We bid you, use your powers and abilities to open paths to experiencing the elementals. Many other people are also working on this. Everyone in their place. If you take up this task, you will have our empowerment and guidance.

The figures disappear again. They surprise me. All the elemental beings I have experienced prior to this have a form appropriate to their realm of responsibility. The water being of a leaf is very small; the faun of a tree is much bigger. This is different.

The kings of the elemental beings—this seems to me to be the appropriate description—appear small in the imagination and do not present themselves like kings. I only find this out through our conversation. Their physical characteristics do not seem important. Apparently, these elemental kings blow formlessly through the elemental world and only take on a form when necessary in order to be more easily perceived.

During the preparatory phase of any greater undertaking, I am in the habit of paying attention to whether the endeavor is supported by the spiritual world. In hindsight, the endeavors that had the backing of the spiritual world were effective and full of impact, even though the success I expected in the beginning did not always manifest. If there was no clear support, then the going was often rough.

I keep focusing on the mood: my employer is the spiritual world, and this employer gives me missions and sends me into earthly work environments as a temporary worker.

Through this I have learned that very high beings like to come into contact with us. The spiritual world is different from the earthly one in this regard. The head of a big company does not have time to speak to every employee; on the other hand, high angelic beings, highly developed deceased human beings, or the Christ being can contact many individuals simultaneously. Their awareness spreads out like a fountain on all sides. There are no limits to their capacity; therefore, you can always address the highest beings on the highest levels and count on their help without having a bad conscience about taking up their time. So I am not really surprised that these kings of the elementals have now contacted me, but I am still moved and inspired.

It is time. In this moment I decide. It is all perfectly clear in an instant. I will do their bidding. As a first step, I will focus on teaching the meditation courses, and the following steps will develop from there.

Meditation is the foundation for perceiving elemental beings, for perceiving anything spiritual. Only when meditation becomes as normal in our society as eating and drinking can collaborating consciously with the elementals become an everyday affair. In the courses, I can practice perceiving elemental beings with the participants and gather many of my own experiences.

Agnes is on board. Meditation is her thing. She has been meditating since she was a young woman. Our different abilities and motivations complement each other well, and so, we begin organizing our courses.

⁓ 2 ⁓

Vacation in Valun

It is nearly three years after my encounter with the elementals, and the meditation courses are running surprisingly well. Almost every weekend, Agnes and I are teaching in Germany and Switzerland, and many participants have found a path for their own meditation practice.

By now, I have met many more elemental beings and learned much about them and their world. In addition, I have encountered several people who have their own conscious connection to the elementals, and through them, I have been able to enhance and refine my own perceptual paths.

I have not had any further clear contact with the elemental kings. Occasionally, I have thought briefly about them but have not really sought contact as I do not have a real question for them. I am working on fulfilling my promise, discovering one thing after another, and the time is taken up with doing this.

In the autumn of 2006, I give a lecture about elemental beings in the Forum 3 cultural center in Stuttgart, where I meet Anna Kleihues, who helps authors find publishing houses. She asks me if I would like to write a book about this subject. Since this idea is already on my radar, we soon come to an agreement, but I never find time to write. Always on the go, already involved with writing a book on the transformation of the earth, moving, kids, referendum in Hamburg, programming a database—I simply find no peace of mind for the book about elemental beings.

We are now packing the car—bags, tents, air mattresses, books, a camping gas stove. The summer vacation has begun. My sons—Lukas, 14 in a week, and Konrad, just 13—Agnes, and I are on our way to Valun on the Croatian island of Cres in the Mediterranean Sea. We have already been there twice. Valun is a little fishing village. The campground is free of cars and directly on the sea, a manageable world in which much is possible. For children it is a dream; for grown-ups as well. Powerful nature, little tourism, and friends from previous vacations will surely be there again. During this vacation, I want to write every day besides enjoying the sea. I want to finally start writing the book about elemental beings. I am looking forward to it. The book has the provisional title "How to Perceive Elemental Beings."

We drive from south Germany over the mountains to Innsbruck, up the Brenner, and then left onto country roads through the Dolomites. While driving the winding roads, my thoughts wander to the elemental beings and their condition, and I notice that it is not good. Feelings of worry fill my heart. What does this mean? I look inward and notice that the elemental kings are approaching, still a little distant, but clearly in my experience. Feelings are emanating from them.

I have to brake, down to 40 km/hour, a tight 180-degree turn, and this is really not the moment. I cannot concentrate. I am in the middle of driving. We have to postpone this until a better time!

Something else is sounding in my soul. This contact feels like a problem, a crisis, a rescue from a threat, complete engagement required—all sorts of things for which I am not at all prepared. I am on vacation. Finally, three weeks without outer responsibilities and appointments. I want to loosen not weigh down my soul! But I do not think this out loud, as if I could hide it from the elemental kings. They have already disappeared again. It is a very short impression. It is drowned out by other experiences, and I soon forget it.

The journey continues—the expressway down to the Mediterranean, Trieste, Slovakia, the Croatian border, currency exchange, Rijka, getting gas, ice cream, finally Brestova, the ferry station. In front of us lie the sparse mountains of Cres above the sea in the setting sun. There, where you can no longer see anything, is where Valun should be.

⌇ 3 ⌇

The Light Fairy

First day in Valun. The tents are up. I have found a nice spot on a terrace in the woods with lots of shade. I can put up a rain and sun shade. This is very important. The kids have put up their tent a bit farther down. The sun is shining. The sea is warm. Let's go swimming first of all!

One can see the port from the beach on the left and the few houses in the village. The cliffs begin on the other side of the beach. I know them well. How often have I looked at these cliffs.

When I looked in this direction as we departed last year, my eyes became a bit teary. I thought it was because of Valun, the experiences, and the end of the vacation, but now I think it was because of these cliffs—not because of the cliffs themselves, of course, but because of my feelings about them. An emotional connection to stones, plants, and water is always a connection to the elemental beings in them. What is happening in these cliffs on an elemental level?

I swim closer to them. As expected, I experience many earth elementals, smaller and bigger gnomes. In front of one pointy cliff there is a very warm, attractive, homey mood. It takes up the space of approximately four square meters. The more I concentrate on it, the stronger the feeling becomes.

What is it? Probably an elemental being.

To better grasp it, I go through my repertoire of experiences. There is a resonance in my heart chakra, and it has the feeling of an air being. But not a normal air being; no, it is more like a light fairy.

Air and light fairies are closely connected and traditionally put into the same category. Light fairy means that she lives in the light and is responsible for the light in the landscape. In fairy tales, the light beings are called fairies, so I call this beautiful being a light fairy. She feels lovely, attractive, radiant. That is on the feeling level. Which form do I experience? It is not a fixed form but like a cloud radiating out on all sides. Radiance is the essential attribute.

Through this slow, always more exact perceiving and describing, my experience becomes clearer and more differentiated. If I did not proceed in this way, step by step, I would only experience that there is something here, and it would stay diffuse. Concepts are like flashlights. Through them I can see better and in a more differentiated way, but they are also the source of error. Concepts have to be supported by perceptions. When you begin speculating and stop perceiving, then you can fall into error. The perception is always true; only the interpretation of the perception can be wrong if you apply the wrong concepts. I say goodbye to the light fairy and swim on.

The next day I visit her again. I quickly come into the familiar sensation. She shines strongly into my heart, almost too strongly—it is almost a pressure. What is going on here? In holding this question, I experience that the fairy wants to come into my aura. She presses into my left side. She wants to make a home there. This already began last year. The threads were spun then. That is why I was so touched on departing last year.

I have experienced on occasion that elemental beings jump into my aura and come along. Mostly it is only for a few days, then the paths separate again. In a few cases, elemental beings have taken up their permanent residence in my aura and become a steady part of my personality. If I have understood correctly, the fairy wants to take up permanent residence.

I ask myself if I want to grant her request. The light fairy has made a good impression. I do not have a light fairy in my aura yet; at least I do not know of one. Probably some smaller light beings are active in my aura, but I am not clear about this. I only get a fraction of the real elemental world in my conscious experience, while most of the rest of it goes by me.

Through having conscious contact with the light fairy, I could learn a lot from her in the long run. So far, the air and light fairies of nature have been strangers to me. I only ever experience their presence before the communication falters, and I do not come into an inner experience and conversation. With the help of the light fairy I could perhaps get a better connection with and understanding of all air and light fairies. She would thus be a good complement to the other members of my personal elemental being team.

The beings that are always around me have special characteristics and capabilities. But I do not want to impose any kind of force on her from my end. The light fairy can try it out and leave anytime she wants, so I give in to her wishes. I observe how I now have the same sensation above my left shoulder as I have close to the top of the cliff. The light fairy is active in both places.

Since she really appears to want to stay permanently, I look for an appropriate name in order to talk to her.

I ask, "What is your name?"

Something is formed, but I cannot grasp it properly. When I repeat the question, there is no reaction. I decide to call her Lara. This was the direction it was going in when I couldn't grasp it.

In the next few weeks I can experience her repeatedly. She is there. But I rarely come into a further conversation with her. It is like a silent getting used to one another. I still need to better understand how she senses, and vice versa, so that we can come into further communication.

⊸ 4 ⊱
Experiencing Elemental Beings

How do you experience elemental beings? Can you consciously make it happen? And how do you distinguish between truth and fantasy? These are questions that have preoccupied me for decades. This preoccupation is the background for everything written in this book; therefore, I want to say something about these methodological questions.

Experiencing elemental beings is generally prohibited by mental blocks. These mental blocks tend to come up particularly when you begin with practical exercises. You think your own perceptions are figments of the imagination, or fantasies, and you are so full of mistrust that nothing remains. So right away you throw out the baby with the bathwater.

This is exactly what I did for many years, until I realized that I should have been washing the baby so that it could leave the bath pure and fragrant. What helped me was to think through the methodological questions in a more precise way and to reconfigure the underlying thoughts and beliefs that led to this mistrust.

This mistrust lives in the air of our Western culture, which is based on natural science, and is thus breathed in by all of us. There is something good about it. The passage through the mistrust can lead to an ennobling and purging of your spiritual perceptions. Without mistrust you would take every inner perception for real, even if your own wishes, ideas, and state of being overshadow and distort it.

For me, spiritual experience has become a neutral, everyday affair. There is a method for achieving objectivity of one's experience, so that you can truly speak of spiritual research. This is true for the perception of all spiritual phenomena and beings, for ether forces, angels, the deceased, Christ, and also for elemental beings.

Elemental Beings:
The Feeling Level of the World

What should we focus on if we want to perceive elemental beings? Let's start by getting clear on the fundamental principles.

When we experience something in the world, we always have numerous impressions. We can see, smell, taste, hear, and touch it. We also always experience forces, feelings, mental pictures, and thoughts. When I look at a stone I experience being held; granite induces different feelings from sandstone. With a stone as my object of perception, for example, I have different thoughts from those I have if I am looking at the sea.

There is a central presupposition working in the background that we do not question. We separate our perceptions into inner and outer world. We think of our seeing, touching, smelling, tasting, and hearing impressions as an outer world, independent of ourselves, and we think of all other perceptions, such as feelings, mental pictures, and thoughts, as the reactions of our inner soul world to the outer world. In this way, we divide the field of perception into two realms through a hidden but entrenched belief that prevents us from seeing this separation or from being able to think about it clearly. This resistance to clear thinking shows just how strong this belief is.

As a result of this separation we say, "The feeling I get from the stone is mine not the stone's," but we treat the color of the stone differently, saying, "The color belongs to the stone."

This split into inner and outer worlds of perception makes no sense, because there is no color except if I experience one. The perception of color is never separated from me or my consciousness. Outer and inner do not appear in perception: when seeing, there is an experience of colors and forms but no inner and outer; when feeling, there is an experience of feelings but no inner and outer; when thinking, there is the experience of thinking but no inner and outer.

Consciously reflected self-observation shows that all perceptions are always a uniform process. The concepts of "inner" and "outer" are completely inappropriate here. They do not emerge from the process of perception; they are superimposed upon this process after the fact. You cannot make headway by using these concepts, but to distance yourself from them is also not easy. We have become accustomed to them; they give our soul security.

But if we avoid separating our perceptions into inner and outer realms, both the color and feeling impressions of the stone are of equal importance. We observe that the whole world is woven through with a feeling plane. Whenever we perceive, feelings are also created. If we do not separate into inner and outer, we can say that the feeling belongs to the stone, just as the color, the form, and the solidity belong to the stone. There is a feeling level to the world, and these feelings belong to the things of the world.

With this discussion about the stone we are now already very close to the elemental beings, because the feeling that belongs to the stone does not exist in empty space; it has a carrier. This reveals itself when you hold the feeling meditatively in your awareness, intensifying the feeling in yourself, a feeling that is held by the elemental beings of the stone. So the elementals are the carriers of the feeling level of the world. I cannot think of a more poignant characterization of the elemental beings. They carry the feelings of the world.

Without acknowledging the notion that feelings belong to the world, the concept "elemental being" makes no sense, for if you presuppose that feelings are just internal processes and reactions of the soul, it then appears crazy when someone speaks of experiencing gnomes and fairies in nature and you deduce: *This poor person has a physical defect and can no longer differentiate between inner and outer world and projects their feelings onto nature in the form of elemental beings.*

In this day and age we often encounter this attitude, and it leads us to close our eyes to the elementals. To find a connection with the elemental world, we must take seriously the idea that feelings belong to the world, allowing us to open up to the perception of the elemental beings.

Through the separation of perceptions into inner and outer we have privatized our feelings in modern Western civilization. We think of feelings purely as psychological phenomena, as an expression of our personality. We have thus abolished the elemental beings and suppressed them from our consciousness and culture.

In previous centuries this was not the case. The fairy tales and myths and many traditional rituals show that elemental beings used to be a reality for human beings. It is still the case in other cultures. In South America, Africa, and Asia, elemental beings and other spirits play a large everyday role in the life of the people there. The disappearance of the elemental beings is thus a phenomenon that is limited in time and space in the cultural history of mankind. It is only nearsighted arrogance in Western civilization that ridicules those who believe in elemental beings.

What led us to separate from the elemental beings? What was gained when we did so? It is an important question. There must have been rightful reasons that led to the separation of the inner and outer worlds. What are these reasons? It cannot just be a mistake.

What is the difference between a visual and a feeling impression? The visual experience of the color of the stone seems more objective than the feeling impression of the stone. We learn this through the simple observation that depending on the mood of the day, the feeling impression will vary while the color stays the same. Why is this so?

Here, the concepts "supported by the body" and "body-free" help in my view. Seeing is supported by the eye as an organ of the physical body. For feelings, there is no appropriate organ in the physical body, even if they have many repercussions in the physical body (for example, blushing and crying).

The feeling organ is located in our invisible bodies: the ether and astral bodies. There is a big difference between the physical body and the ether and astral bodies. The physical body is formed more independently of us. It is a gift of God, a gift of the spiritual world. We are hardly involved in the formation of the physical body. All organs grow and function on their own.

On the other hand, we are strongly involved in the formation of our ether and astral bodies. We have a much greater influence on our feelings, habits, and thoughts than on the function of our lungs or heart. The task the spiritual world fulfills in forming our physical body, we ourselves have to fulfill to a much greater degree in our ether and astral bodies. But we cannot do it as well as the spiritual world does in our physical body; therefore, in body-supported perceptions, we experience the selfless purity of the godly spiritual world, whereas in body-free perceptions, our own weaknesses, deficits, attachments, and fears have much more of an impact.

Body-supported perceptions transmit the motherly feeling of comfort and support, whereas body-free perceptions challenge us to support ourselves; thus, it becomes understandable that body-free perceptions need much more self-motivated activity and care on our part than is true of body-supported perceptions. That care consists mainly of keeping the soul selfless and pure, generally and especially at the moment of perception, because, of course, many egotistical feelings flow into us from the depths of our personalities.

Here, it is useful to differentiate between "world-related" and "self-related" feelings. If it is a mere question of sympathy and antipathy (I like this; I don't like that), then we are in the domain of self-related feelings. Through them the needs and underground of the personality express themselves. In this case, you receive information about the personality and hardly anything about the stone or the object of perception.

Both types of perception have their justification. It is only important to differentiate them, or else all gets mingled in a disorienting way and you confuse the feeling perception of the stone with the feeling perception of the personality. In practice, the discernment is not always easy. Every person has both types of feeling at their disposal.

World-related and self-related feelings are both carried by elemental beings: world-related feelings by elemental beings that ensoul the things of the world; self-related feelings by elemental beings that belong to the astral realm of our personality.

We do, of course, have to get used to making the transition from speaking of feelings to speaking of experiencing elemental beings. In our culture, we are always looking for matter or ideas. The thought that, in the end, the whole spiritual world consists of individual spirit beings is still one we mostly shy away from. But this is the reality, and the more you get used to it, the more naturally you can live with it. Conscious, supersensible perception happens in the following four concrete steps.

Instruments of Spiritual Research

1
Preparation

In our normal state of consciousness, we do not have conscious supersensible experiences, only subconscious ones. To have supersensible experiences, it is always necessary to heighten the concentration and awareness. A regular meditation practice is necessary for this. With heightened awareness, one connects to a higher plane and activates powers of the higher self. In the preparatory phase, it is necessary to form the vessel for the voyage into the elemental and spiritual world. For this, you need ordered thinking, initiative, equanimity of soul, positivity, and openness.

To distinguish whether a supersensible perception flows to you from your personality or from a spiritual being, it is important to learn to see yourself from the outside. In this self-encounter, you meet your own impure, earthbound aspects of soul. The more you can see and take these on with love, the more you will be able to free yourself of them and the more you will become aware that these earthbound soul aspects block the perception of the spiritual world because they tie up awareness.

Only through accepting and transforming these soul aspects can your consciousness enter the spiritual world. In anthroposophy, these impure soul aspects taken together are called the "guardian of the threshold." The confrontation with the guardian of the threshold is a continual, gradual process. In my experience you are never finished with it; rather, ever new layers and themes are always coming to the surface.

2
Imaginative Insight

The first, and for most people the simplest, supersensible mode of cognition is the imagination. In order to make the invisible visible in imagination, we first need to produce an indicator. Much is possible here, including: forms, pictures, mental pictures, thoughts, gestures, words, chakra awareness, awareness of the aura, and so on.

Imaginative insight always begins with an activity of consciousness: we imagine something. The concern of the skeptic that an imaginative insight could just be the product of our own fantasy leads to a dead end. Without fantasy there is no imaginative insight; it only becomes insight if through our own powers of imagination something shows itself, if the spiritual world reacts in some way, and if whatever we put out there takes on a life of its own.

For example, indicators, or tracers, are employed in chemistry. The chemist is faced with the problem that certain substances are invisible, so in order to make them visible, they pour a tracer into the test tube and, depending on the reaction, can determine what the substances are.

This is exactly how I proceed in imaginative insight. For instance, I might produce the mental picture of a square and notice that it adheres to the side of the rock and stays there in a steady and calm way while it fills with many bright, staring eyes. In the meadow, the square acts quite differently, though. It starts moving, the corners wash away, and my mood becomes dreamy. I have to will the square in the meadow to hold its form, whereas, the square on the rock holds its form, even when I am not willing myself to imaginatively perceive it. In a nutshell, this is how I imaginatively perceive earth gnomes that populate the rock and water nymphs that populate the meadow.

Just as the chemist does not necessarily know the meaning of what happens in the test tube, we also do not understand what we perceive imaginatively in and of itself. In order to do so, we either need experiential knowledge or inspiration. Imaginative insight is a rigorous process. I produce different contents of consciousness and observe what happens, then I can draw my conclusions. To make this clearer, below is an imaginative tool kit for the elemental beings in nature:

Type of Elemental Being	General Mood	Chakra Resonance	Conceptual Form
New elemental being	harmony	heart + throat	
Air being	dissolution	heart circumference	
Fire being	ripening	heart + solar plexus	
Water being	movement	heart + sacral chakra	
Earth being	solidity	heart + root chakra	

Three imaginative indicators, or tracers, are described in the chart. **General Mood** is a feeling I create in myself to see how it "fits" the place. **Chakra Resonance** relates to the importance of knowing that the elemental being can touch the heart in an intimate, soulful way; that is why I have written "heart +", as there could be resonance in both the heart and sacral chakras in a place with a water being.

The third indicator is **Conceptual Form**. Earth beings feel at home in triangles, squares, and pentagrams. Triangles match dwarves—it is with good reason that dwarves have pointed hats in fairy tales. Squares match earth gnomes, and pentagrams match house elementals. The form of earth beings is static, whereas, the form for water beings is moving, which can be represented as a fixed point with a circulating point around. You can also find this basic gesture in fairy tales in which nymphs are depicted: on top, the fixed form of the female body; underneath, the flowing fish tail. The form for the fire beings is also moving; there is, however, a powerful waking-up moment in the crossing point of the figure of eight. With air beings, we no longer have the flowing gesture, but rather, a sudden start and then dispersal. With the new elemental beings, the vertical (force of uprightness) and the horizontal (being spread out) are important. You can think of these forms in front of you, or place yourself into the form with your whole body.

Why do these forms work as instruments of perception? When we imagine something, we always create an etheric form. The substance out of which thoughts and concepts are formed is the etheric force. Elemental beings have an etheric body, so these forms either match their form or not, which you can clearly experience.

This toolkit was inspired by the work of Rudolf Steiner and Wolfgang Schneider, and I have happily worked with it for a long time. It has helped me classify my experiences. As an overview, it offers both advantages and disadvantages, for the world of elemental beings is, of course, much more complex than can be grasped through this rough schematic. Our imaginative perceptions are thus an offering we make so that spiritual beings can express themselves and we can perceive them.

Some imaginative perceptions form by themselves without any prompting from me. I described one such imaginative perception in discussing the figures of the elemental kings. Because these kings actively sought to contact me, it required little effort on my part for me to imaginatively perceive them. I saw their form without having to find it slowly through trial and error. The elemental kings came toward me in such a powerful way that upon entering my soul realm they themselves created the appropriate imaginative perception.

3
Inspired Cognition

The experience of imaginative perception is like looking from the outside in: an I–it relationship. Inspired cognition, on the other hand, is like a personal conversation: an I–you relationship.

I go from imaginative perception to inspired cognition by sticking with the inner feelings, willpower, and activities that were necessary for me to produce the images, rather than focusing on the images themselves. This inner shift allows a conversation with the beings to commence. Through inspired cognition, it becomes clear what kind of being I am dealing with. The inspired conversation with elemental beings is mostly nonverbal. They do not speak German or English.

Let me offer an example of how this works.

In my imaginative perception I form a square, through which the gnome of the stone comes into my experience. Now I take away the mental picture of the square, and concentrate on the sensations associated with the square. These sensations are magnified because my attention is no longer focused on maintaining my perception of the square. I live fully in my heart, and notice how a heart exchange starts happening with the gnome. I ask the gnome what he is doing, and this intensifies my experience of the stone and my love for the stone. This is the answer of the gnome who holds together this stone, who is the being of the stone, who fully devotes himself to pursuing his task and is completely satisfied with it.

Some elemental beings are used to communicating with humans and deliver word-related thought and feeling gestures that can very easily be translated into language. With these elemental beings you get the impression that the communication goes via the word.

A key to inspired cognition is tranquility and listening. If I am only ever talking myself, then the being I am trying to contact does not have much of a chance. This being needs an open, quiet soul space in order to speak.

Imaginative perception and inspired cognition are not separate in practice, but rather, flow one into the other. Mainly imaginative perceptions are accompanied by inspired perceptions that you might not recognize as inspired perceptions, leaving you with the belief that you have none. In my experience, you also soon reach boundaries with inspired perceptions, for inspired perception is built on relationship.

The relationship with an elemental being is similar to meeting another human being. To begin with you see them from the outside. Only after living with them will more of the inner self be revealed. Likewise, with an elemental being, in the beginning you only know it is there; to know more, a longer process of acquaintance is necessary. Inspired perceptions are better and more differentiated with familiar elemental beings than with new acquaintances, with whom the conversation is often short. Elemental beings do not engage in small talk, so to have a deeper conversation I need to have a closer relationship.

4
Intuitive Cognition

With intuitive cognition, I take away the inner inspired activity, stay awake, jolt myself back "outside," and identify with the spiritual being, experiencing its life, organization, and connection to the spirit world. I disappear, and only the being with whom

I now identify remains. I see the world through the eyes of this being. It takes me inside it. One intuitive perception that is central to us is our experience of being an "I"; with intuitive cognition, we experience other beings through the "I". The intuitive experience is always an "I" relationship. It is more intimate than inspired perception, and to my knowledge also less common, because it is harder to create the necessary soul conditions.

If you are hearing about these three levels of cognition for the first time, they may seem strange and inaccessible, but this changes as you get used to working with them. In fact, using instruments of perception for spiritual research is well known to human beings, for we all have imaginative, inspired, and intuitive perceptions regularly in our normal lives; we are just not conscious of doing so. To my knowledge, anyone working consciously with supersensible perception works with these levels, even if they do not formulate it as such.

I have separated imaginative, inspired, and intuitive cognition in a clear conceptual way in this description. In practice, they intermingle most of the time.

How Do I Arrive at Objectivity in Spiritual Experience?

When it comes to this question, the following points appear important to me:

- In spiritual experience, the human being is themself the organ of perception. Just as physicists clean their instruments in the laboratory and pay attention to the temperature and humidity, it is equally necessary to constantly keep yourself clean and stay in shape. For this a regular meditation practice, inner purification, and work for soul balance are required. It is important to practice concentration of thought, equanimity of feeling, constancy of will, openness, and positivity.

- In concrete perception, maintaining lack of intention is paramount, for intention covers or distorts perception. If I myself want something, then the being cannot make itself heard. I try with every spiritual perception to test if I am truly in an unintentional space. Here I am always a little skeptical, for I know that in the depths of soul, much is hiding that could interfere.

- Crucial is an experience of evidence, a feeling of truth. We know this experience of evidence from every physical sense perception. That there is a floor here I do not need to prove, for I see and touch it and experience the truth directly; likewise, in spiritual experiences we should have this experience of evidence, this feeling of truth. There are spiritual experiences that feel false. This should motivate me to look at them more closely.

- Communication with others is indispensable. In principle, elemental beings can be perceived in a similar way by all who have trained themselves in this direction. If I say that a big water being has its focus at this specific location, this should also be experienceable by others. In practice, this cannot always be achieved. We are all still in the beginning stages of the cultivation of our spiritual organs of perception. The best training occurs when we communicate with others and meet in person to help transfer skills between colleagues. Communication prevents one-sided and false interpretations. The quality of every scientific endeavor is built on communication between scientists.

- In spiritual science this is also the case. Only through bringing information together and comparing experiences can a whole picture be created, for naturally, everyone, through their human constitution, life experience, conceptual upbringing, karma, and so on, has their specific point of perception. You get closer to the truth the more viewpoints you take into account. Objectivity is not created through negation of subjectivity but through taking into account and incorporating the subjective standpoint.

- In natural science, you often want to create objectivity by getting rid of the human being and, for instance, only relying on technical measuring instruments; however, a measuring instrument is also subjective and only delivers information from its particular position. In spiritual research, it is wholly impossible to push aside the human being, for the human is themself the only instrument of perception. You get closest to objectivity if you are aware of your subjective limits and try to incorporate other standpoints.

- I find the comparison with other places and times very helpful and practical. Spiritual experiences are often subtle and hard to grasp. Only if I try to have the same experience at a different location can I usually clarify my experience. Also, I like to try to come into a spiritual perception on different days to exclude the influence of the mood of the day.

- Results of spiritual perception are in principle repeatable and verifiable, but there are limits to this. In order to repeat an experience, you need to be able to reproduce the same conditions as the original. The more complicated and specific the experiences, the more difficult this becomes. Being able to repeat an experience is also not random, because individual spiritual entities create specific spiritual experiences, and perhaps an elemental being or angel is not interested in repeating the experience to satisfy the criteria of natural science.

- Continual spiritual scientific study and refining of concepts seem indispensable to me—only with refined concepts are refined perceptions possible. If I only have the concept "energy" or "vibration," then I will only be able to experience "energy." Only if I can conceptually differentiate between ether force, elemental being, angel, the deceased, and Christ can I then also perceive these differences. It is no different in the physical world. An enthusiastic specialist can discover so much more than the dabbling amateur will ever notice.

- Of course, assured spiritual experiences only come about through experience, and years of practice allow an inner map to be created. You can grasp experiences in a clearer way and put them in perspective because you have already seen a lot. When you first experience something spiritual you are often excited, but it is better to stay calm. Routine creates calmness.

This concludes our short overview of the methodological questions regarding the perception of elemental beings.

The biggest problem facing spiritual research is that it is relatively unestablished in our culture. The natural sciences engage thousands of professors and billions of dollars in research, and natural science is a subject in school. Spiritual research, on the other hand, does not even exist in public consciousness. If you are working on this you are often looked at askance. The ostracized nature of spiritual research means that it is hard to find the courage to take it up. We make methodological concessions or hide the spiritual behind words that sound scientific. As a result of these missing structures, the potentials and resources of scientific research are not properly used.

Where should someone turn to receive an education in this domain? We lack connective networks, educational possibilities, spiritual scientific congresses, libraries, and research projects. In order for a spiritual impulse to find root in everyday life and ripen, it needs to be chewed through by many people and internalized, and we must receive training in perceptive possibilities. It is my dream to create a Foundation for Spiritual Research to make this a reality. I hope someday to find people who can and want to contribute the necessary funding for such an endeavor.

～ 5 ～

Cres Giants

The types of nature elemental beings that exist are immeasurable. Biologists and botanists have been working for centuries on classifying the animal and plant kingdoms and are always discovering new species. In my estimation, the biodiversity of nature elementals is greater still. As every landscape has a special mood, you also find special elementals that hold this mood.

Here at Cres, my sons play volleyball, eat ice cream, and go diving. After a few days of settling in, everything is flowing well. They have made friends with other children and keep themselves occupied until late at night.

I am sitting in the sun on a rock, looking at the elemental world. What do I notice in particular? Above the sea many medium-sized water beings are dancing. In front of the cliffs and farther out on the sea it is more sparsely populated. The water beings apparently love children at play and relaxed adults and like to communicate with their feeling aura.

In the middle of the beach, there is a big, majestic, bright, crystal-clear Christ elemental being that spreads harmony, well-being, and benevolence. Now I understand why this beach is cozier compared with the other beaches.

I concentrate on the rocks and stones and soon feel myself looked at by many eyes: a myriad of joyfully productive gnomes.

I now focus on the landscape angel, and soon experience myself merged spiritually with every corner, every plant, every house, every stone. The landscape is the body of the landscape angel, which feels part of everything and has everything in its consciousness. In the same way that every person has an angel that accompanies them, so every landscape has an angel. If you want to find out something about a landscape, it is wise to contact the landscape angel. It knows everything and is the highest authority on the landscape.

Apparently, I am in contact with the landscape angel. But I want to test it and ask where it has its focus. My feeling–touching gaze is pulled toward the sea in the port. Yes, indeed, here I can experience a mighty funnel opening upwards with a strong angelic energy. A mighty angel!

I ask further if it can show me an ether source. This is a common etheric organ of the landscape. Ether force streams out of the depths of the earth like a fountain and spreads into the environment, providing it with life force. The angel reacts immediately and shows me a place on the harbor dock. There I feel myself flooded with ether force. I thank the angel and ask if it wants to show me something in particular.

Again, I immediately receive an impulse, and my gaze is drawn to a place at the entrance of the campground. My first experience is of something rough, a force, a being held together. I stay in open awareness at the place, but am suddenly pushed back by a kind of muscleman. Is this just the rough shell surrounding a soft center, or is he truly like this? How much space does he take up? What form does he have?

Keeping these questions in mind, I am astounded when I find this energy in a space about 10 meters wide. It rises like a column, about 100 meters—no, even farther, perhaps 200 meters up! What is this? Instead of thinking, I warm my heart and send radiant energy his way. Perhaps he will reveal more of himself this way.

Slowly, a flow of the heart begins, and I come into contact. Yes, it is an elemental being, but of a kind I have never before experienced. Despite his brusqueness, I gradually perceive him better. He has a forming power over the whole landscape and seems to be the chief around here.

If I think of the main categories of earth, water, fire, air, light, and Christ elemental beings, he fits in with the earth elementals, but he is wholly different from the earth elementals I know so far. He has a strong independent being, identifies with his history, seems ancient, is strong and mighty, and almost has human features. Is it really an elemental being, or was he perhaps created through human deeds? How could I describe him? I search for a word. "Cres Giant!" Yes, this is a being you would perhaps call a giant in fairy tales. I have never experienced one before. The contact weakens. I say goodbye.

A few hours later I go on an excursion. At a lookout point with a view of the mountainous island and the sea, the giant of Valun comes back to mind. Will I perhaps find some giants here as well?

Wow, indeed, there is another one of these giants, even bigger and more majestic than the first! A heart connection is quickly established. Either this one is more accessible, or I have learned so much already through the prior meeting that I can now match the frequency more easily. My connection and ability to melt into the giant are so strong that an inner conversation becomes possible, a conversation in feelings and pictures. I ask and hold myself in meditative stillness, and the answers form in my soul—not completely on their own, of course; instead, these answers flow to me from the giant, and I can experience that clearly.

The only problem is the other tourists. Again, a car has stopped. Would I take a picture of them? Yes, certainly. A man and two women pose in front of the panoramic view. One woman looks at her watch, says thank you. The car doors close. They are gone.

Dear giant, excuse me. I am back. Where were we? Behind me, a camper van puts on the brake. The doors open. Two barking poodles jump out and spread a terrible restlessness. A second car stops. A fat man poses between me and the giant. *Click.* Then all are gone again.

Why can't they just quietly stay and enjoy the view? It is so wonderful here! Why are they all busy taking a second-rate photo instead of breathing in the fantastic original? Who is going to look at all these photos? What is to become of humanity?

Stop! I already almost lost the connection to the giant. I am not responsible for the photos and am not in the mood for depressing thoughts. Stop! It must all mean something and will turn out okay in the end. And I succeed in producing a few nice feelings.

The conversation with the giant continues.

The whole island of Cres is populated by giants. There are many. They have been here a long time, many thousands of years. It is "their" island. They are the biggest elemental beings here, know each other well, and live together like a family. They only live on Cres; they are not interested in other regions. Deep inside the etheric earth they have a meeting point, an etheric cave. Each giant has a powerline to this cave, so the giant family is in close contact with each other. The giant takes me along the powerline into the depths of the earth and shows me the cave. It seems to be very cozy. It also seems empty. Or was there a giant somewhere? I do not know exactly. This visit was so brief that I hardly had time to look around.

When I ask how the giant was created, he becomes transparent, and I come into a high angelic realm. I conclude from this that the giants, like all the other nature elementals, are created by the deeds of angels. The people today find them strange, not understandable, like foreign bodies. They have a very good contact with the other nature beings of the island, however, and these beings have accommodated themselves to the power structure of the giants and integrated themselves into it.

That concludes my conversation. An hour later, I discover the third giant above the city of Cres.

Now I understand the secret of the island of Cres. When you leave the ferry, you feel like you are in another world—barren, mighty, distant times as in the Scottish Highlands, very different from the mainland and the other islands of the Adria. Now I understand how Cres manages to create such an indescribable mood. It is the Cres giants. When you leave the ferry, the Cres giants take you in their arms.

⁓⁓

Two days later, I visit the giant at the lookout point again. Theoretically, each place on Earth is connected to an elemental being: you only need to think of it and open your heart; the ether and astral world is not a spatial world. But if I am unfamiliar with a being, I cannot do this from a distance; my experience is too thin and unreliable, and I cannot get a clear connection. At the giant's physical focal point, I have many more perceptions and can find the soul path to the giant more easily.

I experience the giant as warmer and friendlier this time. The relationship is closer, and the feeling of distance has waned. After a bit of warming up, I ask him about the cave, and if he could show the cave to me again, as the first time was so short.

My experience changes, and now I experience the whole island. Before that I was just in the region around the overlook; now I permeate the whole island from the inside, as if I were carrying Cres.

For me, this means that the giant family holds Cres together energetically. Since I was taken into the center of the giant family, I can participate in their doing this. The cave is comfortably warm. It is not empty. It is filled by a dignified giant radiating an accepting, motherly atmosphere. This mother giant seems to always be sitting here. She is apparently the center or heart of the giant family and of the island. After a while of being permeated with this atmosphere, we say goodbye and go back up.

I ask the giant when he last had such direct contact with a human being? The giant reflects for a moment: *It was a long time ago, about four or five hundred years ago. He always sat back there praying*—he points to the hills above the city port of Cres—*a fine man. He was radiant, surrounded by angels, and gave us many good forces. That was the last human being that spoke to us consciously and communicated with us. Since then humans have become closed and distant.*

~11℃ ℃11~

I travel farther south on the island to see the village of Beley. Soon, I again discover a giant in a meadow. He is already informed about my encounters with his brothers. The paths of communication evidently work well in this family.

I ask this giant if he would like to show me something special? The giant guides my glance to a fir tree. The space in front of the tree is soul-filled, dense, and joyful. What is it? It is the mood of a dwarf approximately one and a half meters wide. But what does it look like?

I have to laugh. I know exactly that something is wrong but cannot put my finger on what it is. I never experience fully formed imaginative perceptions; they are always only indications, with a few percent accuracy. It is not like a photograph, but rather like a modern painting with gestures and color moods. Figures are only indicated with several lines. The imaginative picture on its own is not important to me. It only becomes meaningful through the surrounding environment of feelings, forces, thoughts, and reactions in my chakras and in my aura, through changes in my self-perception and state of mind. My imaginative perception of this dwarf is only sketched with a few lines but underlined with very clear feelings. I know something is wrong but cannot determine what it is.

The dwarf is happy that I am so happy, and so it goes back and forth several times.

I have had enough now, say goodbye, and want to return to the car. Suddenly, the dwarf pulls on me and indicates that it wants to come along. I reflect briefly. There is still a little room in my aura, and this dwarf will be a funny companion. *Okay, come along, if you are not needed here.* So the dwarf jumps into my aura and gets into the car with me. It drives with me to the campground and enjoys itself there in the coming days.

In the evening, I become aware of what is wrong with the dwarf. The beards of German dwarves, if they have one, grow downward. My new dwarf friend also has a beard, even a big one, but it grows upward toward the sky. To all sides, hairs bend upward. Of course, it is my imaginative perception: dwarves do not have a physical form and also no beards. But this image fits the experience well.

The question now poses itself: Do all dwarves on Cres have beards that grow upward into the sky? I decide to take a closer look at the dwarf. Where is it? Oh yes, in front of the entrance to the tent. Just as I had expected: now the beard is gone! It is a dwarf just as I know them.

What happened?

Elemental beings can densify into imaginative pictures and take on different forms. They can dress up, so to speak. When the giant made me aware of the dwarf, the dwarf focused strongly on the beard that was growing up toward the sky, identified itself with the form, and was happy about this idea. Normally, I am satisfied with my diffuse imaginative perceptions, but not this time. I think it was because the dwarf, through its powers of concentration, came into pictorial form in a stronger way than usual and I noticed that my imaginative abilities were not adequate to perceive what the dwarf was trying to show me.

~\ 6 /~
The Elemental Beings of Nature

Elemental beings are quite different from us humans. They live in another world. For me, it is very important to find out as much as possible about them, because if you do not understand another's situation, a meeting is difficult. The study of elemental beings is, of course, a vast field of research.

What are the basics? What should you definitely know in order to understand the world of the elementals?

The living quarters of elemental beings are the ether and astral worlds. The ether world is the world of formative forces, the world's energy. The ether world is very important for us. For everything physically sensible, all matter swims in the ether world and is formed out of this ether world. Our physical body is embedded in an etheric body. When you die, the physical body cannot hold itself on its own and decomposes. It receives its life from the etheric body. In the etheric body you find all life processes. Illnesses appear in the etheric body before they manifest in the physical body. Asian medicine often works directly with the etheric body, as do many Western naturopaths. Healing hands bring the ether to flow again in the patient. Homeopathy works less out of the material aspect of the plant; rather, it bases itself on the information and energy in the plant. It does not matter that there is no physical remnant of the plant in the potentized remedy; it is about retrieving the life force from the plant.

The etheric body is easy to experience. Everyone knows the sensation of someone coming too close physically. You only want to have *friends* within a circumference of 30 centimeters. Why? Because the etheric body usually extends about this distance from the physical body. With good friends, you have an etheric exchange, anyway, so it is alright if they sit directly in your etheric body. With strangers or unsympathetic people, the energy flow is blocked; therefore, you do not want to have these people in your etheric body.

You can touch your etheric body with your hands. For this, it is necessary to first become aware of your etheric body, because you can only ever perceive like with like.

As a basic exercise you can let the palms of your hands approach each other until you feel a resistance, like cotton wool or a tingling resistance in the space between your hands. Being sensitized in this way, you can then feel the etheric body of a human or a plant. If you have practiced this, you can even choose your food products in this way. For instance, organic, natural, and healthy food has a bigger ether aura than artificially cultivated vegetables grown to a certain size.

The etheric body is also the realm in which we create our thoughts and mental pictures. A thought densifies when it comes into the etheric body from spiritual spheres. We can then perceive it. We can also enter the ether world through perceiving the force field around the thought realm and meditating on the question, *What are my thoughts and mental pictures made of?* The etheric body is very flexible and always in transformation. Through concentration you can expand or contract it. What you think about intensely, you turn into etherically.

Our whole landscape is permeated by ether force. This force is different from region to region. Geomancers investigate the ether form of a landscape, a house, or a room and know the different ether organs. Ley lines are like the etheric nervous system of the landscape, from which information can spread out. In the past, castles and churches were often built on them.

The ether is the substance out of which elemental beings are made. If I touch the ether aura of a plant, then I am stroking a nymph or a sylph. If I touch the ether aura of a stone, then I am stroking a gnome. If I touch the etheric body of a human, then I am stroking the group of elementals that belong to that person.

Elemental beings can regulate the ether world because they also live on a higher plane. A higher spiritual plane always affects a lower plane.

The astral plane is the totality of all elemental beings in their manifold forms. It is more subtle than the ether plane. Here you are no longer dealing with forces but with sensations and experiences.

In sleep, our astral body separates from our etheric and physical bodies. Etheric and physical bodies stay together—we are only sleeping, and not yet dead. In sleep, we lose consciousness. After awakening, we often have the feeling that much has happened during the night, and we might remember some dreams. The astral body has not dissolved during the night, but was together with the "I" outside the etheric and physical bodies, where it has done a lot and was renewed by the angels. When the astral body and the "I" reenter the etheric and physical bodies, we awaken and our conscious life begins. That is the main change when we awaken in the morning. We owe our ability to have experiences and to have consciousness to the astral body.

In our feelings, we are closest to the astral body. A thought is formed in the etheric body; it is experienced and felt in the astral body. Without the astral body, we could not experience our thoughts. You can experience your astral body in your auric field if you pay attention to how it feels when someone approaches closer than about a meter. Usually, you will have the feeling that the person has just entered your sphere. The astral plane is the level of experience and feeling. In essence, elemental beings consist of experience and feeling. They are, so to speak, "pure experience." That is why meeting elemental beings is so intense.

In order to properly understand elemental beings, you also need to look at the level above the astral plane, the real spiritual world. The elementals are beings, but not spirit. Angels, or the true human "I", are spirit. The spiritual world consists of angelic hierarchies, the deceased (whom one can also call "spheric-humans"), and the godly trinity.

Elemental beings are guided by spirit and are always connected to spiritual beings. The elemental beings of a plant are carried by the angel of the plant species. This is also called the group soul, or *deva*, of the plant. The elemental beings of a stone are connected to the angel of the stone. The elemental beings of a landscape are permeated by the landscape angel. The elemental beings of the human body are strengthened by the guardian angel of the human being. The angels encompass the elemental beings and guide them. Just as there is no ether world without an astral world, so there is no astral world without a spiritual world.

The ether and astral worlds are not spatial. Space and time only exist in the physical world. This is not easy to understand in practice, because, in fact, one always experiences specific elemental beings at specific physical locations. In a specific location, you will find an earth being; in a different location, a water being. At the root of the plant, one experiences gnomes at work; on the leaves, nymphs; on the flowers, sylphs.

Are the elemental beings not spatial after all? I don't believe so; instead, I think the ether, astral, and spiritual worlds get reflected in space. In these worlds there is no space, but there are different tasks and different stages of development and connections among beings. These tasks, stages of development, and connections are reflected onto the physical world and onto different locations.

My understanding of how this all works comes from mind maps and family constellation work. In mind maps, thought connections are drawn on paper. Slowly the paper fills, and every thought finds its proper place. In family constellation work, the family network is shown in space through representatives that take up positions around the room. One notices if two people should be standing close or far away from each other, turned toward or away from each other. The connections among thoughts and the connections among family members are not spatial in and of themselves, just like elemental beings are not, but they can be mirrored into space. Space and the formation of the earth are actually a kind of "family constellation" of the elemental and spirit beings.

In geomancy, you therefore do not say, "Here stands an angel or elemental being," but rather, "Here an angel or elemental being has its focus." Focus means: This is where the being is concentrated, here you can experience it, here you can connect to it. Also very helpful for me is the idea that the angels live in the cosmic, spiritual world and look down at us from there. Their glance thus falls on a specific location, and I can experience this glance and let myself be seized by the angel.

Since elemental beings are not spatial beings, they also do not look a certain way. They do not live in a world of appearances. A dwarf does not have a pointed hat; a mermaid does not have a fish tail. All pictorial renderings of elemental beings are approximations. Instead of a picture of a dwarf, you could compose a piece of music, write a mathematical formula, or create the choreography of a dance to express its essence. The dwarf should never be confused with its representation. A dwarf does not look like a dwarf but feels like how a well-painted dwarf feels.

The pictures in fairy tales are mostly quite accurate, but they are only pictures. Through our being connected to the earth, we have a great longing for mental pictures that are down to earth. This is a problem because elemental beings are not earthly beings. In my experience, the door to the elemental world is often closed because we have the wrong expectations and wait in vain to see a being with a pointed hat running around. Because of this expectation, we do not pay attention to other perceptions. We are not helping the elemental being if we have this attitude, because we press them into preformed pictures. It is much better to give space to the elemental being to form their own picture of themself.

Since the elementals do not live in space, they do not experience space and the physical world but the ether and astral worlds. When an elemental being looks at a human being, it experiences their feelings, thoughts, moods, intentions, and life energy. What we first see in a human being, the physical body, the elemental being does not see at all. If a dwarf moves through the inner layers of the earth it does not experience matter; instead, it experiences changes in atmosphere. It feels the different rock strata and metals and experiences the spiritual beings and planetary influences that are connected to all of these. Dwarves do not need to build tunnels in order to move through the earth layers, because for them there is no matter.

This is a reason for many problems of communication. We humans often do not understand elemental beings because our concepts and feelings are imprinted by the physical realm. We can start to sense the different world views of the human and the elemental being by trying to identify with those of fish, birds, or earthworms. How does the world look to them? How would an earthworm describe the world, or a fish or a bird? Elemental beings are even more different from us humans than these animal forms. In order to enter the world of the elementals, we need to ignore the physical world entirely and become aware of what remains when we have done this.

Elemental beings are the "being" of things. The gnome of the stone is the "being" of the stone. The house elemental is the "being" of the house. They are completely fulfilled by their respective tasks, and know everything about their domain and care about the details. They are like the craftsmen of the cosmos.

Who are the site managers? These are the big, guiding elementals.

Who are the architects? They are the angels.

Who is the master builder? This is the godly trinity.

I find this description concise, aptly capturing the distribution of roles.

~~·℃ ℈·~~

The nature elemental beings have a differentiated hierarchical structure. I would like to characterize this structure in four groups.

1
The Small Workers

Small workers are everywhere. If I focus on colors in my soul perception, I experience small, one-millimeter big, tadpole-like elemental beings that vibrate differently depending on the color. If I bring the ground into my soul focus, I experience masses of hand-sized gnomes looking at me. If I take the light and brightness into my soul observation, little radiant sylphs flash at me and are immediately gone. If I focus on the gas lantern in my soul observation, I soon arrive at the elemental being of the lamp that feels shackled by the lamp. If I focus on a blade of grass in my soul observation, I experience a water being the size of my hand.

These little workers are the forces of nature. Natural scientists investigating the forces of nature are investigating the habits of these little elemental beings. Physicists and chemists are in reality behavioral scientists of elemental beings. Isn't that a funny thought!

I have long asked myself, *What is matter?* Whenever I go into matter with my awareness, I come to a gnome. In a stone it is often a bigger, well-formed, round gnome, open for communication. In the metal leg of a chair I initially come to the being of the leg of the chair, then I work my way through the material realm and find very small, pointed gnomes; they have little self-consciousness, and instead, are filled by a superior metal being. How the elemental world creates the different materials of matter is a vast, barely explored field of research.

I have only ever found elemental beings on the inside of matter. For me, it is therefore evident that the reality of matter is the elemental world, but how the transition from ether to matter works precisely, I do not understand.

That is why I once asked a gnome I had befriended exactly this question. How do you create matter? Its answer was surprising. It dismissed it completely. It knew no matter and did not create any; it was simply responsible for the stone. And with that, it did not mean the material of the stone but the ether structure, in the middle of which it was sitting, that it was holding together and giving the stone its solidity.

I was not much more enlightened but at least now knew that it is not only gnomes that are responsible for matter. They apparently do not even know that matter is created through their doing but think they are solely concerned with the ether world, so other beings have to be involved that I cannot perceive.

I searched for ideas from Rudolf Steiner about how matter is created. He describes how high angel hierarchies and ahrimanic beings work together in a complicated way to create matter. How it works exactly is another great field of research for the future.

The elementals that have to do with plant growth are impressive. Gnomes, nymphs, sylphs, and salamanders work on plants, each with a different task, often not at the same time, dependent on the phase of vegetation. No, I did not express this correctly—the phases of vegetation are caused by shifts in the different groups of elemental beings.

These joyful little workers can enliven you, but communication with them is limited in my experience. More often than not, they do not react to human attention, have only limited consciousness, and you can only speak with them about their direct task area, if at all. But we owe them our special thanks. Without these unassuming little workers, no law of natural science would work, no plant would grow, nothing material would be held together.

2
The Medium-Sized Elemental Beings

Middle-sized elemental beings, between half a meter to several meters in size, are more eager to have contact with us. They mostly enjoy human attention. They are more conscious, more flexible, and you can converse about more complex themes with them. When I talk about size, I mean the spatial dimension in which you can feel them.

In my experience, these middle-sized elemental beings always have a leading role. They surround and hold together a flock of small workers. Normally, you will find leading elemental beings in every room: a bigger earth being for all the little gnomes, a bigger water being for all the little nymphs, and so on. I usually discover an extra room elemental, the consciousness of the room. They often appear to me like a butler, almost the shape of a human, and belong to the earth beings; likewise, in every garden or park are leading garden or park elementals. The elemental world is strictly hierarchical, almost like a bureaucracy; the difference being that all elementals are highly motivated.

Every tree has its faun. This faun encompasses the big flock of elementals that enliven and ensoul the tree. Fauns are particularly fond of contact. That is why many people have an intimate heart connection to trees. A faun has a lot to do. It holds the connection to the myriad of little workers in the leaves, branches, and roots. It is connected to the group soul of its species, to the archetypal oak or the archetypal fir. It is connected to its diverse elemental surroundings, as well as to other fauns and elementals of all kinds. It is also connected to Pan, a high, leading plant being. Very important too is its relationship to the landscape angel. You see what a dense network of communication the faun is bound up in.

Teamwork is not a problem in the elemental world, for unlike us humans, elementals have no will or ambition of their own. They are completely fulfilled by their task and satisfied with it. In the course of time, elemental beings develop and learn more. Sometimes they get new, more challenging jobs. I often ask myself how old elementals become. I know ancient ones that were created at a time when the earth was not yet solid. And then there are those that are a hundred years or only a few years old. The categories Birth and Death make no sense with regard to the elementals. These concepts only apply to humans. It is better to speak of coming into being, transforming, and going out of existence.

Of course, I wanted to know how elementals are created. Whenever I asked this question, I was led to the working of an angel. Rudolf Steiner formulates it well when he says elementals are "tied up and separated out" aspects of angels.

You can find the little workers everywhere. The density of the medium-sized elemental beings varies, however. You can find houses, gardens, and places that are almost overflowing, also the opposite: abandoned houses, abandoned regions. Middle-sized elementals react to the level of care shown to a place, what mood the humans are in, or how the ether forces flow.

3
The Masters of the Elementals

The third group is composed of the very large elemental beings. The biggest I know take up a circumference of several hundred meters. Surely, there are even larger ones. They take care of the middle-sized elementals and are responsible for larger landscapes or cities. I often experience especially dignified elemental masters around mountain tops or above the sea. Sometimes, it is hard to tell if it isn't an angel; they are so highly developed, so wise and strong.

Compared with these master elementals I often feel the size of an ant. The communication is not as excited as with the middle-sized elementals. The elemental masters are often ancient, have lived with humans for decades or centuries, and oversee great networks of time, so they take everything a bit more in their stride.

The Cres giants, whom I just befriended, belong to this group. I am also deeply connected to the elementals holding the landscape mood of the Allgäu (the region between Lake Constance and Munich in south Germany). When in contact with one of them, my soul permeates the landscape of the Allgäu, above and below the ground. I am inside every hill, mountain, and lake. I notice that the Allgäuer, like the Cres giants, build a network over the region and can be found in many places; for instance, in Eschach to the left of the top of the ski lift, or in Bolgengrath near Grasgehren, about 150 meters beneath the peak. The Allgäu elementals are not big like the Cres giants, generally about 10 meters wide and 15 meters high.

In my imagination, I experience them as old mountain farmers, with felt hats and beards mixed with mountain pine, gnarly roots, and the scent of the Allgäu. The smell impression is always quite strong with the Allgäuer. When I am in the Allgäu, I sometimes awaken refreshed and know I have spent another enjoyable night with the Allgäuer without knowing what we did exactly.

One could also include the majestic, stately Pans, the leading plant elementals among the elemental masters. You often find these in treetops, on the shoulders of the faun of the tree, as it were.

4
The Elemental Kings

Above the masters, we find the beings I have called the elemental kings. They work worldwide and manifest least in a specific location or dimension. They are the highest connecting point for all the other elementals.

For the purposes of orientation, it makes sense to designate the nature elementals not only by size but also by element. Traditionally, nature elementals are divided into earth, water, air, and fire beings. The light beings belong to the air beings.

There are earth, water, fire, and air beings of all sizes, very small and very large ones. This division into the four elements conceptually is akin to mammals, fish, and birds in biology. Mice, tigers, elephants, and blue whales are all mammals. You will find similar huge differences inside the group of earth and water beings.

But do not get hung up on physical characteristics, for fire beings are not only where something is burning. You will also find water beings in places where there is no water. It is not about the outer water; a water being can be characterized by the fact that his soul qualities resemble to some degree those of water. The physical aggregate state is itself a consequence of the work of the little elemental workers.

Since the turn of the century these four categories are no longer enough. For something special has happened. Our earth has been populated by a new, fifth group of elemental being, the Christ elemental beings.

~⫞ **7** ⫞~

Christ Elemental Beings

I was made aware of this new fifth group of elemental beings in 2003 by geomancers Wolfgang Schneider and Fritz Bachmann, and a third geomancer, Marco Pogacnik, wrote and spoke about them as well. These three and other geomancers observed that the new elemental beings appeared just before the turn of the 21st century.

I practice perceiving these new elemental beings regularly and could make the following observation: I find them everywhere, in almost every park, every street, and every room. On the beach in Valun, there is also a very nice one that I like taking a soul bath in.

These new elemental beings belong to the nature elementals and fit in well. It is like a new group of instruments in an orchestra altering the total sound of the elemental world. Wolfgang Schneider told me that with the arrival of these new elementals the old ones changed; they became more awake, more conscious, and more well rounded. I myself could not compare the before and after.

I usually experience the new elementals in this way: They exude harmony, liberating mildness, goodness, and holiness in the landscape. They also have a soothing, freeing, balancing, and healing effect on the human soul. My heart is always strongly spoken to, the front and back heart chakra equally. The throat chakra is often addressed as well. I feel as if my chest and neck were wrapped in cotton wool. Their movement gesture is the vertical, being held upright, and also the horizontal, being spread out across the landscape. Their substance is sometimes gold or white, thicker or airier, depending on the individual elemental being. If I look etherically, I experience their etheric form like an upright, shiny oval.

Several times, I have experienced a new elemental being standing there, as if wrapped up. Only through a heart-to-heart meeting and being spoken to could it unfold and expand. I understand that these elemental beings want to be activated through human beings. They are an offering of the spiritual world, but we must also extend a hand.

I was able to visit several of these elementals regularly over the course of a few years (in Hamburg on the outer Alster, in Kempten, and in the seminar houses of Rüspe and Quellhof) and experienced that they doubled or even quadrupled their spatial perimeter over time. In Hamburg and Kempten, they take up a space of approximately 200 square meters now. If this continues, in a few years' time, everything will be taken up by these beings! I cannot say if this expansion came about due to the nature of these elementals or if it is the effect of more frequent human contact.

I frequently asked these elementals, "Where did you come from?" And I was always then guided to a region that I can only describe as consisting of the substance of Christ. They are evidently not the deeds of angels, like the other nature elementals, but the direct deeds of Christ.

Other changes were noted by geomancers at the turn of the 21st century: new ether forces, new landscape organs, changes in the angelic world, new faculties of supersensible perception in humans, and so on. These changes—all pointing in the direction of a more spiritual future and the dissolution of old patterns—fall under the heading Transformation of the Earth. The new elementals are a part of this overall occurrence.

You can find further background information for understanding these new elementals in the works of Rudolf Steiner, who, in 1911, predicted their coming at the turn of the century (for more information, see his lecture on September 19, 1911, GA 130, p. 30 ff). Rudolf Steiner sees these new elemental beings in the context of what he calls the "reappearance of the Christ in the etheric." Steiner emphasized over and over again that the appearance of the Christ in the etheric is the most important occurrence of the 20th century and marks a turning point in the development toward a spiritualized Earth in the future. One outcome is the new faculty of supersensible perception now common in human beings. This Christianization of the ether world must also be carried by nature. For this, the new elementals are responsible. They are the elemental representatives of the Christ in the ether world.[1]

Since the "new" elemental beings will no longer be "new" in a few years, they need a new name. I find the designation "Christ elemental being" most appropriate, for through this term, the reason for their creation and their meaning is precisely characterized. I hope this name will be taken up in the future.

When speaking of Christ here, I should note that this has nothing to do with the belief systems of denominational Christianity. Christ is a real spiritual being, whom you can experience supersensibly. This being works worldwide and across the cosmos. There are, of course, also Christ elementals in non-Christian countries.

In the fall of 2004, I went to see a eurythmy performance in Bremen given by the Eurythmy Spring Valley Ensemble from upstate New York. Eurythmy is a spiritual movement art rooted in anthroposophy. As the group performed eurythmy to a Steiner text, I experienced the creation of an elemental, which shot toward me, slipped into my aura, and I felt another layer permeating me. This elemental was one of the new Christ elemental

---

[1] On the theme of the transformation of the earth, I edited a collection of experiential accounts by 41 different authors. In it, you will find a comprehensive collection and evaluation of what Rudolf Steiner calls the reappearance of Christ in the etheric. Hans-Joachim Aderhold and Thomas Mayer (editors), *Erlebnis Erdwandlung: Accounts and Texts of Contemporaries,* Borchen: Möllmann Verlag, 2008.

beings and has been my constant companion ever since. I simply call him Christi. I always find him toward the front right side, about 70 centimeters inside my aura.

Through Christi, I can experience Christ elemental beings more easily in nature. I just become aware of how Christi reacts. If he melts into the place, I am probably dealing with a Christ elemental being; if not, it is most likely a different being. Above all, Christi helps me maintain my inner equilibrium. He is always harmonious and in good spirits, especially in precarious or spiritually dangerous situations. It is very helpful to have such a cool companion.

My understanding of how he was created is as follows: Eurythmy strives to be a container for the spiritual world, so Christ was able to enter at that moment and a Christ elemental was created. Since I was probably the only person in the auditorium who perceived this, and because I still had room in my aura, he came to me.

Christi has been on my elemental being team ever since. Lara, the light fairy, has recently joined. Who else is on this team?

⤙ 8 ⤚

The Cinnamon One

ooking back, I had my first clear and conscious elemental being experience in 1998, when I was living in Munich and working on the Let's Free Munich from Debt: For Citizen Participation and Transparency in the City Budget citizens' initiative I had begun.

In Porto Alegre, Brazil, thousands participate in deciding city budget allocations and in many Swiss municipalities, the citizens decide directly about the tax rate and public expenses through referendums, but in Germany, budgetary matters are strictly the province of bureaucrats and politicians. In this country, citizens are left out in the cold, excluded from responsibility and learning processes, and any attempts to change this unhealthy social convention, put in place by a century-old culture of bureaucracy and hierarchy, meet a brick wall.

In short, our citizens' initiative was years ahead of its time (that is why it would eventually be unsuccessful, but I didn't know this yet). I was nevertheless full of enthusiasm and wanted to have a go at getting it passed. To have a referendum in Munich, you need to collect 30,000 signatures. My group of co-workers was very small, and I myself went out onto the streets and into market squares collecting signatures.

In order to use the time meaningfully, I meditated briefly in the breaks before the next passerby approached. The mood alone in various places in Munich was a rich and inexhaustible field for exercises of soul perception. At the Rotkreuzplatz (Place of the Red Cross), I noticed for the first time that a being had been accompanying me the whole day while I was collecting signatures. Sometimes it just hung out in a comfortable way, then it would approach pedestrians coming toward me, wave at them, permeate them, and try to direct them toward me. It was apparent that this being was trying to improve my hourly signature quota.

At first, I only had the vague feeling that some sort of being was there, but if I concentrated on it, I tasted and smelled cinnamon—not physical cinnamon, of course, but soul cinnamon, an experience of cinnamon. If I focused on color inwardly, I got yellow-brown. If I went onto a pictorial level inwardly, I saw something shaggy—a mixture of pieces of fur, hair, and cloths hanging down on all sides. I could not really see a face, and its form was never really solid. If I tried to look at the exact spot where I sensed the being, it would dissolve and melt away. It was as if the being was giving me a picture of a shaggy appearance but also did not want me to fix this image too literally.

This being stayed with me every day, and I could always experience and observe it. At one point, I called it "the Cinnamon One."

In the past, I had had unique, strong, inspiring experiences with etheric forces, angels, and the deceased, but they were always acts of grace. I knew that my meditation exercises somehow contributed to them, but I could not willingly put myself into an inner state that would bring on a spiritual experience. I always experienced it as a gift that I did not quite know how I had received. I had the impression that individual spiritual beings came toward me with huge steps.

With the Cinnamon One, though, things were different. I could be on the tram traveling to a shopping center, putting on the sandwich board with the posters, carrying two scribbling pads, talking to passersby about the referendum, and concentrate on the Cinnamon One and experience him. Apparently, it lay within my control: the Cinnamon One was always around, and I could always find a path to him.

But then I got conjunctivitis from overwork, and the daily collecting of signatures came to an end. And one day, I could not find the Cinnamon One anymore! Even if I inwardly did as I always did, it did not lead to a perception. Had he gone? Had I lost my ability to perceive? I didn't know. I looked back wistfully on our encounters of the last months.

What kind of a being was he? Since he mainly appeared during the collecting of signatures, I thought he was a helping spirit of the referendum.

It did not once occur to me to just ask the Cinnamon One to come back. I thought of "inspired knowledge" as all sorts of things, but not something I could simply try out. Years later, during a geomancy seminar, I learned that our body also has its elemental being, just as every tree has its faun, and realized that, of course, the Cinnamon One is my body elemental!

I once more pay attention to the Cinnamon One and have found the path to experience him again. The fastest way today is if I feel into his home dwelling place, about 70 centimeters diagonally to the left in front of me, and come into a heart connection and feel and taste him. I consciously say *home dwelling place,* because he can move in space; sometimes he is a few meters away, sometimes he surrounds me completely. But via his home abode, I can always find the connection to him.

My 1988 theory that he was a helper for the referendum was false, and this wrong attribution is a typical problem when it comes to spiritual experiences.

In order to orient yourself in the spiritual world you need comparisons. The more beings you know and the richer your experience is, the easier it is to classify experiences. This is quite an everyday thing, not dissimilar to any earthly vocation. In the beginning, you find the inner path to one or perhaps two beings. Everything else is hidden. With such a limited view, it is of course difficult to orient yourself. Imagine you can only see cows and not any other animals; you could easily mistake a camel for a cow!

With time and practice, you become more flexible and these problems of orientation diminish. You become certain about some beings, but in the end, your orientation problem remains, because the spiritual world is extremely rich and differentiated and there is always more to discover.

Back to the Cinnamon One.

He is always around me, participates in everything, carries everything, and is extremely faithful. He is the most faithful and constant elemental being I know. I often ask myself, *What is he really doing?* I usually see him sitting around, relaxing, and rarely being active. But I always have the feeling that this is just an outer illusion. Even if he enjoys his life, in the background he is very active and carries great responsibility. But there is a veil over this. I just see the ragged one. If I ask him directly about this, I never get a proper response. He just stays mute, as if it were ineffable.

I come to experience that he is responsible for the physical body. If I build up a heart connection to him and open up to him with my whole body, then I am more awake. If he appears cut off, and obstructing veils arise between my body and him, then I feel listless and tired. He carries and permeates the physical body and leads and coordinates the many smaller elementals that work in the individual organs and bodily locations.

With simple illnesses or small injuries, I always receive helpful information from him. For instance, I once sprained my ankle, could hardly walk, was in pain, and thought that maybe I had broken something. I asked the Cinnamon One. He showed me that he could not properly permeate the foot, that the etheric aura was blocked in the region of the foot due to angry thoughts I had had. So I dealt with these negative elementals and worked on the ether aura of the foot mentally and with my hand. I experienced a freeing, releasing drainage like draining pus from a wound. The foot no longer hurt as much, and it healed normally. By talking to the Cinnamon One, I could get rid of an energetic block.

In 2006, I began an amalgam detox to free my body of mercury dental fillings. The healing practitioner I consulted on this occasion did a kinesiological test. I had to lie down and raise my right arm. The healing practitioner put certain substances behind me, asked specific questions inwardly and then pushed down on my arm. Sometimes it went down easily, sometimes it stayed up, sometimes it relaxed, and sometimes it tensed. The range of reactions was astonishing.

The healing practitioner arrived at a clear diagnosis and treatment plan, and of course, I was eager to find out what was going on and experienced the following: The Cinnamon One was in a state of high concentration, focused on my right arm, so he hardly had time to respond to my inward gaze and greeting. The tool of kinesiology was allowing the healing practitioner to have a conversation with the Cinnamon One! I observed the same thing during my next appointment.

Two things became clear to me:

First: For every medical treatment, the body elemental being should be consulted, because it knows best what the matter is and what should be done. The body elemental is inside every organ, is responsible for your physical health, and carries every illness. It is the real expert. It is true madness of modern medicine to think one does not need to ask the body elemental being! Of course, such a conversation is not easy. But you can learn through practice. Kinesiology and Bodytalk can help here. To be able to connect to the body elemental of the patient should be a basic ability taught in medical school. Naturally, good doctors and healing practitioners do talk to body elementals in an unconscious way, gain information from them, and then you say that they are talented or have good intuition. In the future, it will be our task to consciously cultivate these conversations.

Second: The Cinnamon One spoke in quite a detailed way with the healing practitioner but not with me! It was clear that when it came to the amalgam detox I was not a worthy dialogue partner, even though I had been in contact with him for years. From this example, an important basic principle of communicating with elemental beings became clear to me. You could think, *Why do we need doctors and healing practitioners if we* *can just ask the body elemental, which knows everything and can prescribe the right medicine? We only then have the problem of the pharmacy accepting the prescription.*

Of course, you should pay attention to the body elemental being, ask its advice, and not act against this advice. But you should not overestimate yourself in this. Conversations with elemental beings are like conversations with humans. I can only understand as much of the other as fits into my horizon of consciousness. If I do not have well-honed concepts, mental pictures, and experiences, the expert in the field can speak with me only in superficial terms—they can't possibly make themself understood with their refined views. I am like a coarse mesh net through which everything falls.

This is the position of the elemental beings. How should the Cinnamon One make clear to me that the sweet water algae *chlorella pyrenoidosa* would be better at the beginning of the treatment, if the concept "sweet water algae" is completely new to me and I do not know the difference between species of algae? The Cinnamon One knows no German or Latin and cannot dictate the words that the pharmacist can then decipher. The Cinnamon One expresses himself in wordless thoughts, pictures, moods, and gestures, so the communication with elemental beings enhances but does not replace the vocational training. A medical doctor can build up special connections to body elemental beings, like a miner to earth elementals, a mechanic to car elementals, a geomancer to the leading elemental beings of a landscape, a housewife to the house elementals. Communication is not a one-way street; it needs effort on both sides.

I can experience the responsibility the Cinnamon One has for my physical body, but I feel he does much more. I always have the vague impression that he is responsible for my whole soul life, all my feelings, thoughts, and impulses, but it stays vague. I cannot experience it clearly or conceptualize it. And the Cinnamon One remains mute. He just does not answer questions that go in this direction.

~◦◦~

Now, in the summer of 2007, in Valun, I search through Rudolf Steiner's 354 books of writings and lectures for what he said about the elemental world. I find a spot where Steiner speaks of our etheric body being carried by an elemental being that is the center of a kind of "solar system." The etheric body elemental is the sun and the myriad elementals that belong to us are like planets orbiting around this central sun. After death, when we cast off our etheric body, we would experience this, and our laid-off etheric body would be attracted to this solar system and become absorbed by it. (For more details, consult Rudolf Steiner, GA 168, lecture in Zürich on December 3, 1916 and lecture in Bern, November 9, 1916.)

This inspired me to do a meditation experiment. For more than 20 years I have been trying to wake up to pure consciousness in meditation. By this, I mean the sphere out of which thoughts, feelings, impulses, and perceptions arise—the sphere underlying these, so to speak.

For this, I need to free myself of my thoughts and feelings, bring this level up, and step into the activity of thinking and perceiving itself. I leave the sphere of thoughts and take a step back into the region of consciousness out of which thoughts are created. I find this to be the basic gesture of meditation and the gateway to the spiritual world, the sphere of the angels, the deceased, the trinity.

A lot is connected to this, and I am aware that this is material for another book. I am aware that it cannot be put into words, ultimately—because words do not reach this spiritual sphere; you can only experience it. If you do not experience it and only hear words, you can only get a vague notion of what is meant. It is similar to music. Descriptions of a concert cannot replace the musical experience.

The awakening to pure consciousness is a death process, a release of the personality, of all memories, of social status, of all specifics of the earthly human experience. At this juncture, I can always experience how strongly I am attached to this earthly life. This attachment turns into a veil that fogs up and darkens everything. The more I detach from my persona—all that defines me as a personality—the more I experience myself as an "I" (this sounds paradoxical, but is so) and enter into an experience of the periphery. I am no longer a point, but become a peripheral being. It is like a turning inside out.

The words "death process" are meant quite literally, for the deceased go through a similar process in their afterlife, according to my experience. When you die, you only lose the physical body initially, causing you to leave the sense-perceptible world. Bringing to the fore and casting off your own thoughts, feelings, and memories is what Rudolf Steiner calls casting off the etheric body after the death of the physical body. That is the second death, the death after death.

Until this point, I was always just concerned with holding myself in pure awareness and forgetting my persona. I never asked myself: *What becomes of my persona?* I just noticed that I could easily step back into this persona. My persona is always present at the end of the meditation and pulls me back in. It gets impulses and light through the meditation and is different from before, but strangely enough, for 20 years, I never asked myself what happens to my persona while in the meditative state. Now I want to find out—not in theory but practice. So the meditation experiment consists of observing what happens to my persona while I am stepping into the state of pure awareness. This is no easy matter.

I go to the beach as I do every morning and climb onto the cliffs. In front of me are the wide sea and the blue sky. I look inward. To begin with, I gather myself and experience my uprightness. Then I build up my concentration. I simply take the word "concentration" as an entrypoint. This gives me an impulse, and I soon leave the word and stay in the power of concentration. Then I make an inner move to the source of the power of concentration,

I condense everything until I notice how I change: first, the sense of building a periphery, then a being filled with lightstreams of force and a feeling of dwelling in oneself. Yes, I am now in the light-filled sphere of the spiritual world, but I do not want to perceive more details in this sphere; rather, in this state, I change my focus and look at where I have come from.

It is a perception that I steer with my own impulses of awareness. The first impression is that I am looking into a cosmic wide space; everything becomes enlarged and has air and space, like the sensation of looking into the expanse of the starry heavens. What is it? The next impression is that this cosmic space is filled with cloudlike moving entities. These entities are being coordinated. By whom? Through the whole, there weaves a kind of spiral substance, like the arms of an octopus, connecting and moving the individual clouds. This connecting substance is a consciousness. Who is it? I slowly become filled with a mood that is familiar to me.

It is the mood of the Cinnamon One, without a doubt! The inner quality is the same, only the imaginative picture is different. He is no longer hanging out but is the director of a universe. When he is there, are there also other elementals I know? I go through some of the ones I know and can find them in specific clouds. I then ask for Angar, my special helper elemental. But I cannot find Angar in this ordered system. I am not sure where he is. Then he shoots like a comet through the system, only to leave again on the other side.

The question remains: *What is the relationship between Angar and the Cinnamon One? Does Angar have a special role?* I get no answer to this question and have to let it be. Then I experience several dark entities, like black asteroids. While the other lighter elemental being clouds harmonize with the whole, these asteroids bring a heaviness. What is this?

I put them into my focus and go into them. It becomes clear to me right away that it is something that is connected to my earthly life. What skeletons do I still have in the closet here?

I go farther in and experience that these elementals were created through thoughts and feelings I have had, such as: *Humans on Earth do not have an ear for the spiritual world. One is always running up against walls. It is pointless. In the end, all stays in the personal realm. Nobody wants to cross the threshold to the spiritual world,* and so on. Such thoughts and moods live in me.

I am surprised—because of the poignancy of the experience with the dark asteroids, I would have assumed worse transgressions. But such thoughts carry a lot of weight in the spiritual realm, and the spiritual world is unforgiving; it is solely interested in the thoughts and feelings I generate myself. Even if these thoughts are justified by the reality of the world, this earthly question is of no interest there; it is only of concern what I contribute to the spiritual cosmos, no matter what life situation I find myself in. It is only important what I do. Through going into these asteroids and through accepting them and the lesson they gave me, they become softer and thinner. I lose them. Then I notice that my strength is waning, that I can perceive nothing further, and I make my way back.

At this moment, the Cinnamon One comes to meet me, now as the "loosely hanging one" again, laughing and hugging me. I am still very taken with and silent about all these experiences. But the Cinnamon One laughs at me heartily. I have never experienced him like this!

It's a full and rich laughter, in which much is concealed. A meaningful laughter. A laughter that tells me: *Now you have experienced my reality. For a long time, you did not know me. You always thought I was the "loosely hanging one" and responsible for your body. But I am a lot more and a lot bigger. I am responsible for your whole persona. I organize the elemental universe that constitutes you as a persona in real life. Everything you think, feel, and do you give me in an elemental way and I carry it. When you die, I conserve your elemental universe, so you can continue to work with it in your next life. When you see me directing the elemental universe, you are seeing yourself from the outside, from the perspective of the spiritual world. That is the reality of your persona, in which you have incorporated your I-spirit. As an I-spirit, you live filled with angels, filled by Christ. That is your true core. When you incarnate, you descend into the elemental universe you have created for yourself over many incarnations that I hold together.*

And again, he laughs at me in his cajoling way.

I feel myself pulled this way and that. On the one hand, shamed due to my blindness; shocked by this strong experience of crossing the threshold, by how drastically I could see myself from the outside. On the other hand, this captivating, brotherly laugh! The laugh gains the upper hand. I have to loudly and whole-heartedly laugh myself.

And so we laugh together, the Cinnamon One and I, and I notice that it is a deep laughter, the forming of a bond. The Cinnamon One has revealed himself to me, in his real dimension as a cosmic carrier of my persona. Life cannot continue as before after this experience. When I think of my persona, in which and with which I must live constantly, I now know that this is just the foreground; the background and the truth is the Cinnamon One! And together with him life goes on! We laugh and celebrate and anchor in this holy moment of a common future!

Then I become aware of the physical world again. I am sitting only 20 meters from the beach! What must people think when I suddenly and without visible cause start bursting out laughing? So I control myself and only laugh inwardly and gaze out at the expanse of sea and sky.

I feel a bit under the weather the next few days. I need a period of rest to digest this experience and integrate it. I do not yet know what it will bring, but I know it was a turning point, a restructuring of my internal organization.

I now also know why the Cinnamon One was the first elemental being I experienced. Since he is responsible for all the processes of my etheric body, he is the elemental being responsible for elemental perception. He is the transmission station. He is part of all my perception. That is why he was the first.

~\ 9 /~

Elemental Comet Trail

I reflect on my experience with the Cinnamon One and try to figure it out. The Cinnamon One led me to a further important realm of the elemental beings. I have until now only discussed the elemental beings of nature and of personal friends in my aura; now, I want to discuss the large realm of elementals we humans create (we customarily call nature spirits "elemental beings" and humanly created ones "elementals").

Just as every perception of the world has a feeling level that is carried by elemental beings, every thought, every concept, every impulse has a feeling substrate. The feeling behind a thought also needs a carrier, which we call an "elemental." Since thoughts, concepts, feelings, and impulses are my own deeds, these elementals are my own creation. The tree is not my doing; the elemental beings of a tree were created by angels. A thought is my deed, so here I take on the task of the angels.

I experience thoughts, feelings, and impulses as etheric forms, densified from higher realms of the astral and spiritual worlds. The elemental beings are the beings of the ether and astral world, so when I meditate, I should be able to perceive them as a mental picture or thought.

I want to try it, so I think, *Today we have a beautiful sunny day,* hold this thought, and perceive the now-created form, which is located in my aura about 20 centimeters in front of my head. I try to move this form. Yes, it works. On a whim I send it down to my feet and let it slowly move up again. What can I still perceive? When feeling through this form, I experience width and warmth in my heart, a feeling of being carried and nourished, of peace, satisfaction, and relaxation. When looking at the form imaginatively, two wide pulling movements, like birds gliding, begin to caress me.

Now I try it with another thought, *Lukas and Konrad are on the beach again without having washed the dishes, which was their task.* If I now feel through this thoughtform in a meditative way, I experience dissatisfaction, hopelessness, and overwhelm. If I look at it imaginatively, it looks like a form imploding on itself, with pulsing arrowheads shooting out. I wipe out this feeling again.

Yes, with every thought, feeling, and impulse we create a new elemental that exudes from us. We do this constantly. In that sense, we humans are a giant elemental factory. Everyone produces at least 100,000 a day! Very powerful elementals also live in leading ideas, sensations, and commitments. Their greater power is due to a greater intensity of feeling and will upon creation. We live with these elementals. They are what we designate "our life." We build our personality on them. All our memories are elementals waiting for us to go into them, to enliven them and awaken the memories and bring them back to life.

What happens to the myriad elementals we continually produce? There are two possibilities, according to my understanding: either they are a working part of our personality or they go into a state of dormancy. I have often asked myself if it is possible to dissolve elementals. I believe this is possible and that you can simply wipe out a part of the past, but I do not have any experience with the final dissolution.

Normally, we are less concerned with dissolving elementals than redeeming and taking the energy out of them. If an elemental loses its power, it becomes a bookkeeping reference (this is how it was in the past). Since it is dormant, it moves farther away spatially in the elemental world and finally becomes part of world memory, of the so-called Akashic Record. In the Akashic Record of the ether world, everything that ever happened in the world is inscribed. This is meant figuratively, since it is not a book but an accumulation of countless elementals.

The elementals we have created put a stamp on our surroundings. Individuals differ from each other on a feeling level. We speak about what a person radiates—some people radiate a loving, peaceful mood; others radiate a joyful one; still others have a field of tension around them. According to my understanding, these differences in mood in individuals are created by the different elementals streaming out of them. Depending on the kind of elementals we exude, we attract other elementals. If we are sad, this is amplified by further sadness elementals from the astral plane that we draw in; if we are happy, happiness will also stream to us from our surroundings.

Magicians work a lot with the conscious creation of elementals. Through ritual acts, strong will, and intensity of feeling, they try to create elementals to realize their goals. This is how love magic works, as well as black magic. Magicians put a curse on objects by placing elementals on them; one well-known curse, for example, protected the funeral chambers of the pharaohs in Egypt. What we call a demon or ghost is often an evil elemental. The elemental is not in itself evil; it is only fulfilling the purpose for which it was created. It is not responsible for working the evil; its creator is. Morality and freedom are human concepts and don't fit the elemental world.

The creation of elementals always involves acts of magic. As human beings we are free to act consciously: we can create elementals that obey personal interests and goals that are not in alignment with world goals but also create elementals that support and nourish other beings and harmonize with the life of the world. As a result of this freedom, acts of magic can be white or black. The difference between a white magician and a black magician lies in the motives and intentions associated with their actions. Even if both do exactly the same thing, their individual motives and intentions will lead to white magic and the other to black magic.

What magicians do consciously, we all do unconsciously. For example, I experience people's positive and negative intentions toward me very strongly. When conflict arises, a person only has to have critical thoughts about me to hurt me—they don't have to say a thing. In a fight, it often feels in my imagination like a pack of mad dogs rushing at me, ready to tear me apart. On the other hand, in loving relationships, I have a precise sense of how nourishing and fragrant beings flow to me on a soul level. Sometimes, for instance, I sense a friend is thinking good thoughts about me and is with me. Or I think of someone, and they call!

Of course, what I experience with others, they also experience with me, and I am often shocked. When looking back on what I was feeling and thinking during a moment of conflict, I have been startled to find myself responsible for biting piranhas, pricking cactuses, or stinging jellyfish streaming from me! I prefer the flowers, butterflies, tumbling trolls, or colorful bands of energy I experience when I am in a good mood. There are redeeming or binding elementals, depending on the intention of their creator.

All of these elementals have an effect—they stream to the people to whom I have connected them in thought and either strengthen or weaken them. Often you can notice tension between people of a sympathetic or an unsympathetic kind. What is this tension? It is the elementals. They stream up out of the unconscious into the conscious soul life and show themselves there as an experience of tension. The elementals of a loving couple are very different from those between people whose chemistry does not match.

If a malevolent elemental leaves me, am I then rid of it? Unfortunately, not. It is connected to me. My stamp is on it. In my experience, you can determine who created the elemental from this stamp. Concretely speaking, I experience an elemental in my auric or soul space and have the impression it was sent to me from someone else. If I look at the elemental precisely, I am led to its creator, who becomes visible as if they pop up on a screen.

Since the elementals I create stay connected to me, they will return to me some day, and I will have to acknowledge myself as their creator. So watch out with magic—in the end, it is not worth abusing the magical powers we all have as humans. It is a big riddle to me why black magicians believe they can escape unscathed from their actions. I assume that they are only thinking short term, like a drunk: as long as they are still pouring out the alcohol, we will continue to drink! But at some point, all the evil elementals return, and the black magicians will have to pay bitterly for them.

What is the real difference between good and bad elementals? Every elemental has a connection to the spiritual world. In the spiritual world, we find the angelic hierarchies that live paying homage to the trinity and are suffused by Christ. Angels speak through good elementals. Christ speaks through Christ elemental beings directly. Because of this, good elementals are connected to and nourished by cosmic life. They live in abundance, giving and allowing freely.

There are also spirits in the spiritual world that are not open to the trinity and lead a separate existence. All of these spirits have the fundamental problem that they are not connected to cosmic nourishment, so they are always hungry, sucking, and parasitically binding themselves to a host. Since they cannot live independently, they possess other beings and live at their cost. But you don't find many beings in the universe that allow this to happen to them. Why should an angel filled with Christ let themself be possessed? It would be a very bad trade for them indeed.

In my experience, there is only one group of beings that lets themselves be possessed by these split-off spirits: humans. This has a striking effect on our production of elementals. If we are filled with the normal angelic hierarchies, the elementals we produce have a freeing, nourishing, and good hue. If we are filled with adversarial beings, we produce elementals with a binding, sucking, and evil imprint.

What kinds of adversarial forces are there? The beings Rudolf Steiner differentiates were a big help to my understanding. Steiner describes the adversarial forces with incredible precision and detail.

The spirits of Lucifer comprise the first group. These enclose the soul and give it a being of its own. In connection with Lucifer, the soul takes itself very seriously. First and foremost, it seeks self-realization instead of being filled by spirit. Lucifer wants to sit on Christ's throne. He inspires the soul in a negative way to become egomaniacal, narcissistic, full of indulgence, fleeing the earth. Vain people have strong luciferic elementals in their aura. On the positive side, Lucifer inspires enthusiasm, entrepreneurship, and creativity.

Lucifer literally means "light-bringer" (from the Latin: *lux* = light and *ferre* = bringer). We owe a lot to Lucifer in our culture. It is not about disconnecting from Lucifer but of ennobling him, so that he can become a wonderful helper and friend.

In the spiritual world, there are luciferic angels in all the angelic hierarchies. If a religious or spiritual community has a strong luciferic influence, then a luciferic angel can focus itself in its space. I have experienced this in several churches, but most churches have angels imbued with Christ.

Luciferic spirits fight over possession of the human heart. Like the stranglehold of a snake, they can occupy the heart space and lock up the throat area. If people no longer experience their hearts, then this generally means that Lucifer has absorbed it. The majority of luciferic beings have an orientation point, namely Lucifer himself.

I once came to him by intensely meditating luciferic elementals that someone had produced. These luciferic elementals were connected to luciferic angels, and through them to Lucifer himself. I wanted to engage my will and my power of concentration and pull myself up to him through these connections. It did not work initially, and I had to take it into the night. I woke from sleep and experienced a mighty, strong, rebellious fellow surrounded by red flames. In my experience, he was very big, as big as the universe. That was what was special about him. And because of this, I knew I was on the level of the fundamental spirits of the universe. Lucifer is not a small spirit but about as big as Christ. It was a tremendously exhausting enterprise to withstand the gaze of Lucifer, and I kept thinking his might would kill me and his fire burn me.

The second adversarial group consists of the legions of Ahriman. Ahriman is the spirit of darkness. He is the spirit that negates himself and proclaims he is not a spirit. He loves the darkness, and there is nothing worse for him than to be illuminated by the light of human attention. If I take hold of an ahrimanic being with the power of my consciousness, it winds around in dismay.

Humanity used to be naturally clairvoyant. This has been lost in the last few centuries. Thoughts, feelings, and impulses are no longer experienced as deeds of spiritual beings. How did this happen? The ahrimanic spirits have dimmed human consciousness and have occupied our thinking and perceiving power. They have pulled a black veil over our consciousness.

I got to know Ahriman, in particular, through trying to wake up meditatively in my thinking and perceiving activity. We humans of today live completely in our thought contents, in the results of our thinking activity. But what is the thinking activity itself? What is the perceiving activity? What is our part in it?

In the beginning, it did not seem possible for me to wake up in the activity of thinking and perceiving. I did not know what to reach for. After many years, and several twists of fate, it began to work more frequently, and I noticed that screaming ahrimanic spirits run from me whenever I put myself in the state of witnessing my own consciousness. These ahrimanic spirits had darkened my own connection to myself and made me a captive of the sense world and thought contents. This is how Ahriman tries to shut down the ability of the human soul to access the soul–spiritual world and tie consciousness ever more to the physical body. I could often observe that the aura of human beings who have no access at all to perception in the subtle realms is filled with ahrimanic elementals. In the soul, Ahriman induces feelings of fear and abandonment.

ifer, Ahriman has many good sides, and the task also one of transformation and ennobling. Ahriman icture and form to thought content. Without the ann.. ation of thinking, our modern natural science would not be possible. We also owe our earthly sense experience and its sobriety, clarity, and concreteness to Ahriman.

Without Ahriman in our perceiving activity, we would not have the impression that the sense world is outside, objective, and independent of us. We owe him materialism, technical advances, and commercialization. Our cities are permeated by dark ahrimanic veils, whereas purely natural environments sometimes remain free of these. The many ahrimanic beings have a point of reference, Ahriman himself. He often appeared to me imaginatively like a black hole: nothingness.

The third big group of adversarial beings are the so-called Asuras. These are really vicious. Compared with these, Lucifer and Ahriman are harmless. I experience the asuric beings as pinching, piercing, and shattering. The Asuras eat up the power of the "I" and generate a lack of courage and hopelessness. Elementals carrying feelings of hate and anger are permeated by Asuras. With Lucifer and Ahriman, I have the impression that there is a coherent universal being at the highest level. With the Asuras I find no center; they are all split up.

These three groups of adversarial beings are residents of the spiritual universe. How did they come into being?

Rudolf Steiner concerned himself with this question extensively. He described that the trinity commanded spirits to disconnect from the Godly stream. With this sacrifice, the conditions and the necessary resistance were created so that we humans could develop freedom. With this thought, I can understand a lot of this much better. We have to grapple with Lucifer, Ahriman, and the Asuras. It is a feature of human nature that these adversarial forces work in our soul. It is always a matter of transforming and ennobling them. It is always about finding their positive core. They are like a resistance through which we can find uprightness.

This is different with the forth adversarial group: the beast of the Apocalypse that is called Sorat. Sorat does not inhabit the spiritual universe; he lives outside it. He apparently did not participate in the creation of the spiritual universe but comes from somewhere else. Sorat stands behind the Asuras and the ahrimanic spirits and overshadows these. In my experience, Sorat can only work in the spiritual universe if people bond with him freely. He does not appear naturally in our soul, only if we actively invite him in.

Sorat attracts you through the promise of power. Many black magicians have fallen into this trap. The Asuras are at work in blind anger, Sorat himself in conscious evil deeds. I experienced Sorat imaginatively as an aggressive, snarling, black monster wanting to devour the spiritual universe. Taken by himself outside the spiritual universe, I did not find Sorat evil. He is a strange, incomprehensible, and in some ways even loveable being. He becomes problematic in relationship to human freedom. Sorat is not about transformation but about pushing away and separation.

Whereas all well-intentioned elementals are woven through with the angelic hierarchies or Christ, all evil-intentioned elementals are woven through with adversarial spirits. Lucifer lives in selfish, vain, or hurt feelings. Ahriman lives in cold, materialistic thoughts and feelings of fear and abandonment. The Asuras live in hate and feelings of aggression and the corresponding thought patterns. Sorat lives in conscious evil and the corresponding negative conceptual dogmas. The difference between good and bad elementals thus comes about through the fact that there are normal and split-off spirits, both with their corresponding elementals.

In the course of my life, I thus create a comet trail of elementals. What happens to this trail when I die? In all esoteric teachings you find the description of a purging process happening immediately after death, a kind of moral judgement of the previous life. This phase is also called Kamaloka.

In death we begin to awaken, to be born into the spiritual world, initially on the etheric plane. With this awakening in the elemental world, the whole, self-created comet trail becomes visible. We then see exactly what elementals we have produced in our life, and in looking at these we evaluate ourselves. In this, it is only important what we ourselves have done. The outer causes, the "guilt" of others, become irrelevant.

In this Kamaloka phase of self-knowledge, everyone is confronted by mixed feelings. Much of it is nice to look at, but in every case, there is plenty we do not like and would prefer to correct. But it is impossible to correct after death—we can apparently take the energy out of the elementals we have created only here on Earth. As a deceased person, we cannot reach the soul realm where they were created, which would be necessary to dissolve them.

This central rule of the Kamaloka time is always described in anthroposophical or esoteric literature. I have not fully understood why this is so, but my experience has confirmed it. I have often found deceased individuals suffering from self-created elementals they do not want to accept but cannot get away from. These elementals may have come into being through disparaging thoughts or destructive deeds and remain in the deceased person as long as he does not own and accept them. Sometimes, this is a long process of digestion, and in the acceptance, the will to correct this is born, giving the impulse for the next life: we want to retrieve and redeem bound elementals.

This is my understanding of how karma works. Our past karma consists of specific legions of elementals that wait for us on the astral plane. Our future karma is the elementals we create today. The spiritual world and we in our prenatal state organize our destiny in such a way as to always meet up with the people we have old karma with, where we have old elementals to redeem.

The old karma surfaces in problematic situations, in particular. In a few cases, I have come into conflict with another person and the fight has escalated and is no longer really understandable as related to the situation at hand. Why is the other person reacting so strongly? Why am I also reacting so strongly? The present situation does not justify it. In such situations, I have taken on the habit of meditating on the aggressive energy, of accepting and going into it. This often takes days and sometimes, pictures, feelings, memories, and relationships reveal themselves that do not stem from this present life. The karmic background of the conflict becomes clear and the conflict usually loses its intensity.

How do we explain this?

Somewhere on the astral plane, elementals are waiting that were created in previous lifetimes because I did something immoral or someone did something immoral to me. Now I meet this person in the present incarnation. We begin having a relationship. A common soul space and exchange of elementals is created. The old unredeemed elementals slowly surface and observe the situation. When the right moment comes and the mood is such that they find a resonance, they enter the common soul space and latch onto the current elementals. The conflict now intensifies to match the situation in the last incarnation, where we perhaps had a life-or-death encounter with weapons. Today, we might have a harmless situation in comparison, yet we feel the intensity of "life or death." The old unredeemed elementals want to be lived through again, accepted and redeemed, so that they can enter their well-earned place of peace. If it does not work on this occasion, these elementals wait for the next one.

With these thoughts in the background, much of what I was experiencing in my social surroundings became more understandable to me. Old karma always surfaces—at work, in the club, in the family. It is the nature of the beast that old karma is often dramatic because elementals carrying love and joy are already redeemed and support us while leaving us free. Only negative ones still want to be digested, and therefore push in. With these reflections, it becomes clearer to me what the Cinnamon One is doing for me in holding together and ordering this comet trail.

~∙⦿∙~

The sun has set now. The children have already had supper and are back on the beach with their friends, laughing and playing. I feel tired from the sun, the sea, and the writing. In the tent, next to my air mattress, is my box of books. On top is a book by Daskalos, the Cyprian healer and master. Daskalos means "master." His real and difficult-to-pronounce name is Dr. Stylianos Atteshlis.

It occurs to me that human-created elementals are Daskalos's life theme. As a healer he worked mainly with these. Through working with elementals, he cured the illnesses and psychic problems of thousands and encouraged us to take care of our elemental inner world. This was of utmost importance to him.

I open his book *The Esoteric Practice: Christian Meditations and Exercises* and read the following lines:

> Our present personality is the sum total of the elementals we have ourselves produced or have taken over from the common psychonoetic atmosphere. Elementals are taken into our character and build our constitution. The growth of our present personality starts before birth with the habits and preferences that we bring from previous lives. The personality develops throughout our lifetime and through every experience; in this it solves some problems and creates new hindrances for this and the coming lives.
>
> Eighty percent of our thinking and doing are conditioned by our unconscious wishes and desires. We are only seldomly conscious of the origin of our wishes and yet they dictate a lot of what we experience and determine to what degree we enjoy life or suffer. These desires and wishes are in reality groups of elementals that we always nourish with etheric vitality when we act to satisfy their cravings.
>
> This does not mean that something subconscious is "bad" or "good," because for most people it is a bit of both. The subconscious is both unavoidable and of infinite value and can

be your best friend if you allow it to give expression to sacred–spiritual intelligence—or your worst enemy if it is dominated by base desires and unbridled emotions.

The subconscious, and the personality in general, can be measured in terms of quantity and quality. Elementals can be evaluated and even counted. Most of our elementals serve egotistical purposes instead of helping to better the common selfhood. The largest number of problems we encounter result from reawakening base elementals.

Masters also have a subconscious. But in the case of masters the subconscious is smaller compared to their degree of self-consciousness, above and beyond which they have incorporated qualities like love and compassion into their subconscious. If we were to compare the subconscious of an average person with a polluted jungle, the more evolved humans have shaped their subconscious into a peaceful meadow. And if a gardener takes care of his garden, the garden will take care of the gardener.

The looking within is a serious effort to lift up our subconscious into the light of self-consciousness and become more conscious of our motives and activities. This is a process of purification of the subconscious, with the goal of getting to know ourselves better and increasingly becoming the master of what we think, feel, wish for, and do. We should strive to take care that the elementals making up our personality are guided by love, insight, and right thinking.[2]

These words summarize everything so nicely! I take Daskalos words into the night.

---

2 From Daskalos, *The Esoteric Practice: Christian Meditations and Exercises*, 1994.

Social and Machine Elementals

Without social beings there would be no social life. I spend almost every weekend at a different seminar house, Waldorf school, or other institution. How different the moods are! Of course, they are related to the different houses and landscapes, but they are also related to the specific community.

Every community has a definite atmosphere and is unique in its manners and behaviors. I have often experienced that people are different at work than at home. Institutions leave a mark on individuals. Why? Many complex processes are at work here that create a group entity in the elemental world. This collective entity permeates the individuals and influences them.

I have often had the following experience: I have a person in front of me. They are an individual, but now the group entity is working through them, so they are only partly an individual now. I also know the following experience: I have a person in front of me. Even though they are permeated by the group entity, they are an individual. Their individuality is carried by the group entity, which in fact strengthens them. There are collective entities that strongly influence the individual, and there are ones that leave a lot of free space for the individuality of the person to appear. I think we should try to attract the latter kind.

In my experience, elemental beings are created in all social settings that carry the mood of the collective. Of course, the collective entity depends on the tapestry of elementals created by the members composing this collective, and the collective entities are connected to the angels that have been attracted to these groups of people. There are very high, sincere, and wise ones, but also cruder ones holding more tension. Changes in communities always bring about a change in the group entities as well.

It is very interesting to observe social processes or gatherings from the elemental perspective. Here, you can pay attention to different aspects. Is there a group entity in the room? Which elementals do individual people exude? How is the group entity in regard to the whole? How do the elementals change in the course of a meeting? How is the group entity changed? What other entities join in? I could occasionally experience that in the course of a meeting a big social elemental out of cosmic depths joined, built up a power and a mood, then disappeared again.

Friendship also attracts a friendship being that holds the common soul space. The feeling of connectedness is an elemental. If a friendship ends, you sooner or later find no more connection between you. What was so close and intimate has suddenly disappeared! How is this possible? According to my perception, the common friendship being has pulled away.

Machines as well are inhabited by elemental beings. I experience this most clearly with computers. The computer reacts very sensitively to the moods and attitudes of the users. I was responsible for the computers in the office of More Democracy. I would often get an exasperated call that the programs were no longer working. I would have a look, and as soon as I sat down in front of the keyboard everything worked perfectly. I believe the cause was the exasperated, insecure attitude of soul of the frustrated co-worker. This caused unpleasant elementals to flow into the computer, confusing it.

Machine beings influence the functioning of machines. If the machine being is well, the machine runs better. If the machine being is weighed down by bad human feelings and thoughts, then a malfunction occurs. The love of the machine is an important factor. A workshop student once told me there were continual problems with a big machine at his workplace. If he put his attention on these problems, the machine would begin to function well again. If he then concerned himself with his actual task again, the machine would start malfunctioning again. He looked for the cause of this for a long time and only found that the worker that was assigned to this machine did not love it.

~⊀ 11 ⊁~

Angar: An Old Friend

In the course of our incarnations we meet some people over and over. This can also be true of elemental beings. Angar showed me this. I met him in August 2005; rather, I met him again, as I was shown during the course of the meeting.

Back then I was on vacation with Lukas, Konrad, and Agnes in Bonfin, south of Nice in southern France. Bonfin is home to the international meditation center of the Fraternité Blanche (White Brotherhood), founded by Bulgarians Mikhael Aivanhov (1900–1986) and his teacher Peter Deunov (1864–1944), two of the most significant European spiritual masters of the 20th century.

I see them as representatives of esoteric Christianity. Their work is very focused on the human meditative path of schooling. Life in Bonfin is such that vacation and meditative life are connected. They also have a large program for children. The program is mostly for small children, though—Lukas and Konrad found Bonfin a bit boring after a while and did not want to return there; at their age, they preferred the freedom of life in Valun.

Angar is the elemental being with whom I have the most contact and with whom I work the most today. How did I get to know him? Luckily, I captured it exactly in my diary.

August 4, 2005

I want to write something about a new kind of communication: speaking with elemental beings and angels. Until this point, communication was very limited and took a long time, so I stayed in feeling gestures.

The day before yesterday, I tried something new with the earth being who lives on the coast between St. Raphael and

Le Dramont. I tried a mental conversation on the etheric plane using formulated thoughts and taking the etheric form into it.

In preparation, I projected myself into the coastal being, settled down in it, concentrated on pure thinking, paying attention to going into it existentially and without prejudices in a body-free state. When I felt a clear connection to the coastal being, I formulated a question and watched the reaction, the answer. This already comes before the question is completely formulated. The answer comes in the form of a thought that I can then easily translate into words.

Frau von Holstein describes this similarly in the *Flensburger Hefte* and calls the language "etheric."

One can ask: Does the answer really come from an elemental being or out of subconscious regions? I find I get clear answers if I am awake at the moment of receiving the answer and connected to the elementals. There are also answers that I do not experience clearly, so that a feeling of insecurity remains. Now to the conversation with the coastal being in its main points:

What is your task?
I lead the earth beings in the coastal region. My focus is near the big rock on the beach that you know. However, I am not bound to it but able to move freely and whizz through the whole coastal area; for instance, I also work inland.

How were you created?
[I experience pictures of moving angels, and out of this movement this being is created. But I am not sure if this comes out of prior knowledge, so I leave it open, since I cannot come to a clear experience. Later Angar tells me: "It is true that I was created through a pinching off of the angels."]

When were you created?
In the time of Atlantis. Back then, the earth did not have a solid form. Since then I have passed through many stages

of evolution. [I experience the Atlantis times as having a melancholy mood or sound. The earth being takes me there. Everything is etheric and dreamlike.]

Do you know Rudolf Steiner?
Of course! As do many of the deceased. He carries me and the whole cosmos.

Do you know Aivanhov and Bonfin?
Of course! I always send earth beings to Bonfin for rehabilitation. They rejuvenate and receive training there.

What is your relationship to Aivanhov?
He is inside me; I live out of him. [I have the impression the coastal being does not mean a deceased person outside himself, but rather, is pointing inside his own inner being. And there I experience Aivanhov as a specific color tone that I know from his books. This color tone is impersonal in the cosmic periphery.]

What does it mean "I live inside him"?
He is my sustenance. He gives me power and a cosmic footing. Through him I transformed into a new form, a new form of consciousness.

How long has this been the case?
Since his death [Aivanhov died in 1986]. Before that it was already like that but more like a premonition; since his death, it unfolded in its full strength.

Does Aivanhov work on the entire global elemental world or is he confined to a region?
In the spirit world, Aivanhov has a global impact, but the nourishing ground he provides for the elemental world is restricted to the regions he was most active in and incorporated into himself. You will not find Aivanhov inside the elemental world in the region of Allgäu, for instance, but other deceased souls instead. In me as well, you will not only find Aivanhov

but the deceased of the region. Due to his great spiritual dimension, Aivanhov is especially formative and striking.

Do all the deceased have such an impact?
Yes, the deceased shape the landscape via elemental beings. If you go inside the elemental world you come to the sea of the dead.

What is special about Aivanhov as a deceased soul?
He developed cosmic I-consciousness during his lifetime. This light now radiates from him into us and illuminates us elemental beings, spiritualizing us.

What is your hope and expectation of us humans?
We hope that more people on Earth will achieve cosmic consciousness and help us to connect to the Christ.

How do you experience the deceased that are blocked in their development after death and stay caught in the in-between spheres because they were materialists on Earth?
I perceive these. They don't bother me but don´t help me, either. I can stay free of their influence.

Can you take me to other important beings, for instance those near the dragon cliff?
[He takes me with him, but I cannot hold the concentration and sink into dreaminess.]

Will I be able to hold the connection to you in the future? Is there a way to make contact?
[He inscribes a cross into my right shoulder. I do not understand it and ask several times what it means. He repeats it. If I mentally reconstruct this cross, I can connect to him right away. It is a direct connection, a red telephone. I later try thinking of this cross and, indeed, it works!]

Thank you for your cooperation and friendship. I hope and wish for a good collaboration!

Angar: An Old Friend

August 5, 2005

Should I spread the message publicly that the deceased are the nourishing ground for the elemental beings, or was this message only meant for me?

Yes, spread it around. People should hear it because they are the nourishing ground, whether they know it or not. The more this is known in the human realm, the more our conditions improve.

How can I create a secure connection to you?

Pay attention to your heart. You must feel me in your heart, then I can start the conversation. Only ask me serious questions. If it is not a real question, I do not understand it. I do not understand words.

How can I be sure it is you and not another being or my subconscious?

Pay attention to your heart. You have to experience me. Pay attention to your thoughts. The thinking realm should be left completely free and without aim. My answers come quicker than you can formulate the question. They come as a movement of thought. These movements have the sound of my being. In sinking into this movement, you will be guided to me and not to someone else. If you are unsure, then ask. Your powers are limited. Illusions can always creep in out of the surging astral sea.

You are not satisfied with this writing. What is missing?

What you have written is correct but still too vague. You must experience how I create this thinking movement and be present to the moment of creation. This will give you certainty and a feeling of truth. Checking afterwards is also possible but less sure. I recommend you only be satisfied if you experience me as the creator of the thought movement in the present moment. If this is not possible, repeat as often as possible or just stop.

Does it bother you if I write down what you say?

No, but read it to me so I can check it.

Can you show me other beings in this bay?
Look around! [In looking around, I find a water being that I am connected to through the sacral chakra. This is responsible for the bay. I linger a bit with him.]

Tell me about your past. How long have you lived here?
Several thousand years.

What did you do before that?
I sped over waters and seas, but I was a different being then. I look upon him as someone else. Elemental beings transform.

What did you do before then?
I was already an elemental being at the time of Atlantis. Everything was different then. There was no hard earth— everything was etheric, and the densest substance was wafts of fog. Over time, the earth became denser and harder. I served human beings back then. These were also very different from today. They had no I-consciousness, no solid form. They looked like elemental beings and lived with us. The wishes and intentions of humans flowed our way and guided us. We served as machines for buildings, for example. I knew you back then in your incarnation. This is why the connection is relatively simple today. I was your servant, you could say, in those days. [During this response something seared through my aura. I inquired repeatedly. He confirmed it each time.]

What did we do together back then?
I followed you around, but I cannot tell you more. When the time has come for you to recognize your karma, you will find out for yourself.

Tell me more about Aivanhov.
He brought me the most significant transformation and changed my substance. Last night, during the meditation in the big hall in Bonfin, you called me with the sign of the cross, and I showed you how the elemental beings drink in this meditative

substance to empower and transform themselves. The good condition of the elemental world in Bonfin is carried by these daily meditations. [I get the distinct impression that the conversation is finished and ask no further questions.]

August 7, 2005 (In the Afternoon at the Sea: Conversation with the Coastal Being)

Rudolf Steiner describes in the closing lecture of the Christmas conference on January 1, 1924, how many people are caught in materialism and cannot pass the guardian of the threshold at night, because they do not bring any substance that can endure in the spiritual world. If the soul were allowed to pass into the spiritual world, it would be paralyzed and would come back without impulses. But this also means that the human being is not able to pass the guardian of the threshold after death, either, for if they did, they would be reborn as a thoughtless, purely instinctual being (= cultural destruction and barbarism). Steiner bases the Christmas conference and the anthroposophical movement on this insight, so I now ask the coastal being:

After death, what happens to souls that were materialists?
[The conversation with the coastal being is not easy; I was never quite sure who was giving the answers, he or I.] The answers in summary:

- These people stay caught and after death, cannot go on the developmental path until rebirth.
- This type of deceased is not so bad for elemental beings, they root deeper (in the cosmic deceased and the angels).
- As long as there is still one cosmic deceased person, elemental beings remain grounded. If all the deceased were stuck, elemental beings would disintegrate and lose their ground.
- Those deceased who are stuck have a big influence on humans, however, who generally are not rooted deeply in the spirit and are thus exposed.
- It is necessary to start a movement to help the deceased.

To broach another subject with the coastal being, I ask him what other elementals live on the coast. For a moment, the coastal being permeates me and I can look through his eyes and see inner spaces where dwarves dwell instead of the cliffs. This is a tangible experience and reassures and rewards me after the uncertainty I felt during the meeting.

I should practice this method of perception of the elemental world: merge with friendly beings and look through their eyes.

August 8, 2005

In the afternoon, I was tied up with other things and did not converse further with the coastal being.

August 9, 2005

Regarding the coastal being: It wants to come with me and give up its coastal task and help me with my spiritual research. The clear experiences with deceased souls I had this morning were probably also thanks to him.

August 11, 2005

In the afternoon I am on the beach for the last time. I could not get clarity with the coastal being. Even if it comes along—I feel it in my right shoulder—it will stay focused on the cliff by the sea. This was my experience.

I close my diary. This is how I got to know Angar. I notice that it was also my summer vacation. A time freed of outer obligations and demands makes it a lot easier for me to perceive things more clearly.

I had a guilty conscience for a few months, thinking that if Angar stayed in my aura, he would be missing on the coast and I did not want to take anything away from the coast. I also thought that if every tourist did this, then the coast would soon be depopulated of elementals. Initially, I got the impression that he was still connected to the coast and active in both places, then this stopped, and I noticed that he was no longer interested in the coast at all and even happy to give up this task.

A year later, I was back in Bonfin and visited "his" cliff. I found that Angar was no longer focused there. A mild, fragrant angel had taken his place. The cliff is now an angel focus. So I understood: it seems to be part of the divine will that Angar placed himself in my aura. I started calling him Angar—at some point I no longer wanted to call him "the coastal being," because he no longer was one. I asked him if he didn't have a better name.

One time, I wanted to know from Angar why he didn't call on me earlier. Why only when I was 40 years old? Angar guided me to an angel worthy of respect that came imaginatively in front of my eyes. He had commanded this angel to wait for me on the coast. What kind of angel was it? It was not my guardian angel, but one hierarchy higher, an archangel that stands behind my guardian angel. For me this was a concrete experience of how the angel world weaves our destiny.

In the first meetings with Angar, I was enthusiastic about how close to words our communication was. Later, I found out that this is only possible with him, and so far doesn't work with other elemental beings. The speech-like communication works with him because we have been partners for many incarnations. I know him well, and he knows me well. But even with him it often doesn't work if I am not in the proper state of mind or he isn't present.

Angar is not always there. He is often gone, sometimes for weeks, which made me unsure in the beginning, but then he suddenly pops up after a long trip and has much to tell. Sometimes he says he has been at a spa for rejuvenation and "folded himself away." If I ask him what he folds himself into, he always says, "into the higher angel hierarchies," and what resonates along with that always feels really relaxing and healing.

Some of his trips make me feel uncomfortable. For instance, when I grew deeply concerned about the common future of human beings and elementals and the idea of writing a book began to grow inside me, Angar was enthusiastic and energized and sped off for a few days. When he came back, I learned that he had traveled throughout the elemental world and spread the news of my decision to write this book in order to give them a happy, inspiring message, to shake them awake. The reactions had been very different: some were positive and delighted, but some negative. In some places he was chased away like a dog, for enough elementals have been permeated by adversarial spirits to not want to hear of any of this.

I did not like Angar's missionary zeal. I felt like he was overselling things, and it was much too soon. It was only a statement of purpose, and I did not have any concrete ideas or a project yet into which this could flow. Angar had created expectations in the elemental world, and I did not know if and how I could fulfill these, but I realized that Angar's journey had nailed me down. Now I had to do it, as too many eyes were looking my way. Maybe this was the higher sense of his mission.

Angar's flexibility becomes apparent to me over and over again. Even though he is an elemental being, he can evidently travel in all spiritual realms and spheres of the dead. I think that elemental beings are normally limited to certain regions of the astral and spiritual planes, but Angar is different; he has special ability.

When I really need him, he is there. The sign of the cross on the right shoulder works very well. I only use it when it is really important. Often, we have nothing to communicate for weeks. If I make the sign of the cross, then I generally feel the right side of my aura from head to toe being permeated by his substance.

How do I work with him on a practical level?

I trust him; he knows a lot more than I do in supersensible realms. We act in concert, and he is faithful and reliable. In the spiritual world, you are always dealing with individual spirit beings, but many are not suited to giving advice because their perspective is too limited. You have to know what to ask of whom. With Angar I always feel well advised.

A big advantage is that the communication with him is fluid and relatively steady. I do not have this with any other spiritual being. I cannot talk to my angel like this. I can just feel if I am energetically permeated by him or not and draw conclusions from there. Advisory souls from the realm of the dead are sometimes there, and sometimes not. I know that other people have a different experience of this. This is my experience.

Angar is not only my advisor but also my supersensible organ of perception. If I want to perceive elemental beings in my surroundings, I often ask for Angar's help and try to look through his eyes. The intensity of my experience is then enhanced. If I want to feel into places that are located farther away, for instance the hills on the other side of the bay, then I ask Angar to go there. I can then experience the condition of the distant spot imaginatively.

Once, I was confronted with a problematic etheric vortex during an earth healing session. I asked Angar to feel into it and see what was going on there. Full of gusto and fearless he dived right in, was put through the mixer, had trouble coming out, and when he came back to report on his findings, I got the necessary information.

Through Angar, I now understand the shamanic meaning of animal totems. Shamans (medicine men) cultivate a special connection to a specific elemental being that helps them with their work in supersensible worlds. But Angar does not look like an animal. If I go into the plane of imaginative pictures, he has a human shape and is surrounded by a fluttering, shiny cloak.

-\\ **12** /\-

A Concert Visit

It's Friday, August 17, 2007, and tonight, there is a classical concert in Lubenicke, as there is every week in July and August. I get a ride with Roman, a holiday acquaintance from Vienna. An ensemble from Rijka is playing in the little old church. There are eight musicians. Bach and Vivaldi and another composer I don't know are on the program.

I enjoy the music. Immediately, I feel freer and connected to higher realms. My elemental team has come with me. How are the different members of the team reacting to the concert? In the course of the evening I find out.

Lara the Light Fairy is enthusiastic. She is active, expansive, and immersed in the mood of the elementals that live in these pieces. She reacts rapturously and sentimentally to them. I wonder if this is healthy, as it seems like an overreaction to me, but then ask myself, *Why can't I just let Lara's reaction be? Why am I judging it?*

The Cinnamon One is apparently neutral when it comes to music. He is in his peaceful, relaxed mood, focused on his own business, and does not react to the music.

I do not get a clear experience of Christi the Christ elemental. I am not sure I am getting all that she does, but I cannot find a reaction to the music on her part. Instead, she seems to be busy working on a tension between her and the Catholic elementals (we are after all in a Catholic church). Somehow, there is a difference of opinion between the Catholic elementals and Christi about the understanding of the Christ. There are reproaches. But I do not truly understand what is really happening.

Angar is unnerved. He would like some thinking and clarity, not this indulgent music. He would like something real to do. I suggest he investigate the earth beneath Lubenicke if he is getting nothing out of the concert. Angar takes off listlessly and comes back empty-handed after a while. Then the tide turns. The music has attracted several angels, which can be felt in the room. Angar is interested in these and is now communicating with them, so he is getting his money's worth after all.

The reaction of the dwarf that got on board in Beley is impressive. He is with the musicians, waiting next to them, making an important, meaningful, and happy gesture. He evidently wants to be noticed by me. Soon after I notice him, he moves toward the musician playing the violin. This musician joined the others for this piece. He is impressive. His violin has a virtuoso, living sound. What is even more impressive is his inner involvement. He is involved with his soul, his heart, his listening, and his concentration in the music and carries it.

The dwarf positions himself behind this musician, and I can observe how he slowly enters him. He disappears as an independent being and unites with the aura of the violinist. He is now helping him and taking part in his musical experience. What is the dwarf so interested in? Why is he so engaged? I come to the conclusion that he is interested in the transition between the sound of the music and the sound that glides into the etheric.

The members of my team react totally differently. Lara is interested in the elementals of the music, Angar in the angels of the music, the dwarf in the etheric underground of the sound. And I am satisfied with an overall impression of all these regions, together with the sensual hearing experience.

The piece ends, and the first violinist leaves the stage. Instead, an oboist joins the others. How does the dwarf react? I now find him between the three violinists of the ensemble. He is equally connected to all three musicians, not just to one. The dwarf stays there until the end of the concert.

⟿ 13 ⟿
The Crisis Intervention

It is just after eleven at night. The musicians begin their last piece. I no longer concentrate on my elemental companions, but lean back and relax into the sounds of Bach.

I do not even notice how it starts, but all of a sudden, I am in the middle of it. The elemental kings are in the church. I feel surrounded by them and remember our contact being cut off on the way here in the car. Yes, now I am open for the meeting.

If I am seeing it properly, the leading earth, water, fire, air, and light beings are present. Very quickly they get to the point—not in words, but in wordless thoughts and impulses. They are very worried, and I learn the following: The mood is shifting, and morale is sinking. The nature elemental beings of the earth are very disappointed with us humans and feel abandoned. The situation is dire. The elemental kings can no longer tell their entourage that everything will be well.

A few years ago, elemental beings still expressed confidence that conscious co-habitation with humans would start, but nothing much has happened since. More people now know about the existence of elemental beings, but passive consumption of the subject matter has not led to action: hardly anyone is developing the will and love necessary to come into direct contact with the elemental world, and everything depends on nature elementals being seen by humans.

I sense the reproach in all this and feel cornered. Do they really mean this? Why are they so pushy? We still have a long time. This will not happen in a few years. This will take centuries. I take it personally. (*I am already doing what I can—seminars, lectures, book project. What are you complaining to me about?*)

It all goes so quickly that I do not notice that I *am* personally involved. Personal involvement and communication with spirit beings is a contradiction, because when you are personally involved you view the world through rose-tinted glasses. I do not notice this at present, but it will inform and disturb the conversation that follows.

A group of nature elementals is still missing: the Christ elementals. I ask if we should not wait until the representative of the Christ elementals comes? Immediately there is an added nuance, a mildness and goodness full of strength and confidence. This means to me that a representative of the Christ elementals has now joined the discussion.

Suddenly, there is a change in mood. The situation is serious. Everyone is doing what they can. Let us see what we can do practically to bring this situation back into balance. From an accusation we have moved on to the search for solutions.

I try to clarify what this is all about and think the following: The little elementals don't care much about contact with humans. The big ones are sovereign and oversee long periods of time. There should be no problem with these two groups. But the middle-sized elementals are not as stable, since they do not have such a broad perspective and simply feel disregarded. The appearance of the Christ elementals around the turn of the century has raised the confidence of the elementals quite a bit. Presumably, this pool is now used up and needs new deeds to satisfy the impatient middle-sized elementals.

But why is it not possible for the leading elementals to show the middle-sized ones the connections and time perspectives? Why have I not noticed any of this excitement in my own elemental contacts?

But this is no longer the theme. There is no feedback as to whether I have understood this correctly or not. There are no answers to these questions.

It is now simply the question of what one can still do; specifically, what *I* can do. I can no longer distinguish what comes from whom, but to me it seem as though the elemental kings chime in together.

The serious desire to do something has to be stimulated in human beings, they say. If for instance, I call the book I have been working on "How to Experience Elemental Beings," this would be nice but sounds almost like a hobby akin to "How to Learn to Climb." This would not communicate the disregard the elementals feel. The point is to muster a strong desire to respect the elemental beings.

I have objections. Human beings have a hard time experiencing elemental beings. They get in their own way mentally. Even if they have clear experiences, people have untold mental tricks to not believe in themselves. It takes a long time, years or decades, to dismantle this, even with good will. This is my experience. As long as you have no experience of the elementals, the desire to come to their aid cannot arise. How can you stand up for something you have no experience of?

To this they reply: Only if there is love for the elementals and people decide to stand up for the elementals will they be able to perceive them. The will to do so comes first. Without this will, one will never free oneself of the mental and emotional blockages.

This convinces me, but the human will is free. Everyone has to develop their own will. You can do nothing from the outside in this regard.

This is true and needs to be reckoned with, they say. But I could simply describe my own will and, thereby, give people the idea that you can will yourself to stand up for elemental beings.

I have further objections: Of course, I could come out more clearly in this regard but that would push me ever more left field. If you speak about elemental beings, many people look at you askance. Not only is there discrimination against elemental beings but there is discrimination against anyone with supersensible experiences.

I would be free, financially pretty independent, they say, and not aiming for a career of some kind, so it would not be so bad.

I reply: Even if I just speak about this meeting with the elemental kings, who would believe me? I will be looked on as a dreamer. This sounds much too strange to the human ear. If I speak of an elemental in a plant or a landscape, this is already a lot, but still somewhat comprehensible.

Do I mean that they don't exist? Reality is not based upon present human concepts.

No, of course you exist, I say. I experience you in a very real way. But why should I lean myself out of the window to such a degree? There are also many other people who have contact with the elemental world.

This meeting is, however, now taking place with me, they say. Other people are not present here. Everyone is standing at the place assigned to them and fulfill their tasks.

I object further: I am not sure if other people who experience elemental beings are also experiencing that the mood of the nature elementals is shifting. There is probably not a consensus about this, and I am supposed to make this the starting point of my activities?

Of course, not everyone experiences this. Reality has many facets. I should ask myself if my experience is false and double-check.

I continue: Even if I call the book "Plea against Discriminating against Elemental Beings" and work with that, nothing much would be changed. It will take humanity a long time to integrate the elemental world.

It's about generating a strong desire to act. Elemental beings need to experience that humans on Earth are working seriously on their behalf. Only through appropriate deeds can trust be reestablished. Spiritual deeds alone do not suffice; elemental beings need deeds on the physical plane, and generating a strong desire to act and strong deeds among humans would accelerate the cause more than a weak desire and weak deeds.

This goes too far for me. Calming of the elemental beings cannot be dependent on my activities.

I am wrong about this and am being watched. Of course, it is only one building block among many, but other stones could be placed on top of the foundation stone. A more decisive stance could set in motion a force that could affect a lot, more than I would believe.

~◦~

And so it goes, back and forth. It is a difficult and turbulent meeting, and there are many obstacles to overcome, then it ebbs away and the meeting is dispelled.

In the meantime, the concert is over. I applaud. Outside, I have a drink with Roman but still feel preoccupied by the deep experience with the elementals. He asks me what I am thinking about. I cannot tell him all that now. Where would I begin? So we speak of other things.

Afterwards, I am confused by the conversation. I feel the earnest concern of the elemental kings. This is really an important issue, that I have understood. But the background is not really clear to me.

I am now thinking of giving the book the title "Plea against Disrespecting Elemental Beings." I want to represent the position of the elementals in the strongest possible way.

In the coming days, I experience what a difference it makes to the will if you stand fully behind the elemental beings and speak up for their rights. In this the elemental kings are right. It makes a big difference.

~\ **14** /~

Invitation of the Giant

I have to go to Lubenicke today. I have been thinking about it all day. Lubenicke is the old stone village on the western coast of Cres where the cliffs are. Pirates are supposed to have once lived there; today 24 people call it home. The village is based about 500 meters above sea level, and you look almost vertically down to the sea.

Lubenicke is beautiful. I love it. Today is a wonderful, clear, sunny day with a refreshing breeze. Everything is shining, joyful and shimmering—vacation mood in pure form. I write and swim, have a few conversations, play a round of Risk with the children, walk on the beach, gaze at the sea.

Today, a holiday friend of my sons, Sara, is moving into our tent. She will be staying with us for four more days. Josef, her father, is leaving today. My sons and Sara are happy their vacation is continuing; they have been together for days. I do not want to leave until we have said goodbye to Josef.

Today is also restaurant day in Mamalu. We eat there every third day; on the other days, we make meals on the camp stove. This is the deal I made with the kids, and I have to stick to it, so it doesn't make sense to drive to Lubenicke beforehand. I want to have time there. I will drive there later and spend the whole evening there.

But we arrive at the restaurant later than planned and are there so long the sun has almost set by the time we finish. What will I do in Lubenicke at this late hour? It will be dark before I get there, and I will not be able to see even a foot in front of me and will trip over stones. I am thinking now that I would rather go tomorrow, then I will have the peace and quiet I need to make contact with the elemental world and discover what I still need to learn there.

But something decisive arises in me. I should still go there now. I don't know who is calling me, but it is coming from inside my heart, so it must be right. I stop thinking, climb the hill to the car, and drive through the darkness on narrow streets to Lubenicke.

Now what do I do?

Since I am here, I go to the panoramic cliff while there is still some remaining daylight. I hasten up the stone path. As I do so, I look inward for a moment and see that I am much too driven and this will lead to nothing. How am I supposed to come in contact with anything here? How can I achieve inner peace? What is wrong? It doesn't matter. Just go up, first of all.

I sit on the highest point on the cliff wall, on the spot with the telescope, and look around—first across the sea, then to the right over the stone plateau . . . and I almost fall over backwards! Such a mighty force is pushing my way! What is it?

Immediately it becomes clear to me: here, on the highest point of Lubenicke, another Cres giant is standing like a lighthouse. He is mightier, bigger, and more masculine than all the other giants I know. I feel very small compared to him. I look at him reverently.

Everything is moving too fast for me. I have been sitting here only a few seconds and have not even caught my breath. You cannot do this to me! You are overwhelming me.

So I go back 20 meters in order to be able to perceive him with more distance. I pay attention to leaving the experience and becoming free of it. I want to be structured about this. I imagine a wide, high column, the simplified form of a giant, at the spot that just struck me so vividly, then I let go of my power of concentration and observe what happens.

The form is filled by a feeling of power that almost floors me. The form holds, and the column remains standing. Then I imagine the same form onto the cliff plateau in the other direction, and let go. This form is not filled by any feeling; it stays empty and disappears quickly. Then I put the form of the giant in the space above the sea. It does not hold here, either. The form test indicates an elemental being belonging to the species Giant.

Then I concentrate once again on the alleged giant spot and go through my auric sheaths. I do this mainly mentally, but also add my right arm to it for support. In a distance of about 50–70 centimeters, I experience movement and flow. This is the level of the astral body, so the aura test indicates an elemental being as well.

Then I go to the inspiration test and ask, *Are you a giant?*

I inwardly experience a gesture with the singular meaning "Yes."

I ask further, *Do you also have a connection to the giant cave inside the earth of Cres?*

The giant shows me his connection, and I practically see it with my inner eye and experience an echo of the cave, all very briefly.

My standards are now almost satisfied. On this secure foundation I can proceed. I feel myself to be grounded and focused, but a question does come up: How did I come in contact with the giant so fast? This normally takes a longer warm-up time, and I was even in a bad inner disposition. Best to simply ask the giant himself, so I turn towards him:

How did we come into contact so quickly?
The giant: I was waiting for you. I knew you would still come tonight.

How did you know this?
The giant: We invited you.

You invited me?
The giant: Yes, we invited you, not only me.

Why was I invited? We don't even know each other.
The giant: Of course, we know each other. You have been in contact with my giant brothers. We are one family. When you speak to one, you are speaking with all of us.

Why then did not another giant invite me, but you?
The giant: I am more experienced and more practiced in having conversations with humans than the other giants. Don't you notice how well I can make myself understood? I form my answers in gestures and pictures you can easily understand, so I can explain complicated situations to you. You don't need to search for long to translate it into fitting words. This translation is so easy you almost feel like I am talking to you in words. But I do not know human language. I have only observed for a long time the formations occurring in people's etheric body when they speak and think. I try to act the same way.

Yes, I understand you extraordinarily well! This is hardly possible with other elemental beings. What prompted you to invite me?
The giant: The crisis intervention with the elemental kings took place in the church in Lubenicke. I and many other elemental beings were there and heard what was going on.

Then a lot of elemental beings know about what we spoke of?
The giant: Yes, many elemental beings know about it. We naturally observed what consequences this crisis intervention had and are happy that the gravity of our situation is now apparent to you and you have decided to do what you can. But we also observed that there is something blocking your power. The conversation wasn't as good as it could have been.

Yes, I continue to think of the crisis intervention, I still have a big question regarding this. Why is it so terrible for you elemental beings if you are disregarded by humans? You get your strength from the spiritual world, after all. Why cannot you simply say, these humans are momentarily useless, let's just ignore them; at some point they will come around?
The giant: We have observed that you have not rightly understood this. The disregard of humans weighs on us. It is uncomfortable but not really threatening. The large elementals understand the benefit and light we will receive if humans

use their free will to act on our behalf, so they can better handle the disrespect. Little elemental beings, which do not have an overview, suffer more from this. The earnest and worried demeanor of the elemental kings is not because of the disrespect, but because of the consequences of the disrespect. The disrespect is uncomfortable, but the consequences of the disrespect involve our substance and our life.

What do you mean by the consequences of the disrespect?
Now the giant shows me a shocking image. He shows creeping, wolf-like beings lurking and waiting for a chance to attack. This image is accompanied by strong feelings of fear and defenselessness. Then I find myself wanting to replace images with words again.

The giant: When I look around me, I see packs of ahrimanic and luciferic elementals on the prowl. They are hungry. They are parasites by nature, since they are not connected to the cosmic sources of power, so they sneak around us nature elementals, searching for ways to permeate and appropriate us. They want to nourish themselves from our strength and have us serve them.

How do these elementals come into your surroundings?
The giant: These ahrimanic and luciferic elementals are continuously created by humans. They are increasing in number, and in the last decades have been growing exponentially. Ahriman and Lucifer only have access to us through humans, but people don't recognize what streams out of them on an elemental level. They don't know what they create in the world through materialistic and egotistical thoughts, feelings, and deeds, but we elementals can always see the danger creeping around us right in front of our eyes.

But you are not even vulnerable! You are protected through the angelic world and through Christ.
The giant: Right now, I and other nature elementals are safe from attack; our aura is still strong enough that ahrimanic and

luciferic elementals can find no point of entry. But we are all finding that our aura is growing weaker and we are becoming more vulnerable. Today, I am a strong and mighty giant, but if things continue in this way I will fall and become fodder for the pack of hounds.

When will this happen?
The giant: This question is difficult for me. We elementals do not live in time like you humans. We live in a kind of eternal present. In this present, we find ourselves being sacrificed to the ahrimanic and luciferic beings. This has us very worried. Translated into your time, this must still be hundreds or thousands of years away, but we are experiencing it now, and are therefore worried now. I cannot tell you this with any more precision.

Why is your aura getting weaker?
The giant shows me an image of his aura or substance. This actually feels delicate and vulnerable and it becomes clear that it is no longer being filled by the spiritual world as it has been in the past.

The giant: This is because the angelic world is slowly pulling back from us elementals. It used to hold us with a strong hand and protect us. Today, the angels are farther removed and do not protect us nature spirits as before. That is why we have become more vulnerable.

Why do the angels do this?
The giant: The pulling back of the angels has to do with the freedom humans have. Michael, as the leading time spirit, trusts you to be free. Freedom can become the highest and most valuable good of Earth evolution, an ever-radiant light. Freedom can only come about through being let free. That is why the angels leave humans free under the regime of Michael, and consequently, also us elemental beings. To be left free by the angelic world is the prerequisite for freedom. Actual freedom is created when you humans give us nature

104

elementals a base protection in freedom and love. We nature elementals and you humans are in the same boat. Our destiny is interconnected. If you humans fail, you pull us nature elementals into the abyss with you. You humans do not even know about the abyss, but we have it in front of our eyes.

What do we humans have to do to empower you and take away your concerns?
The giant: If you respect us and permeate us with consciousness and love, then you give us protective and holding power. You illuminate, irradiate, and spiritualize us. Through this, you are also connecting us again to the angelic world, because the angels live in human freedom, in the light of your consciousness.

[The giant creates further thought gestures.] This is the serious background of the crisis intervention meeting. The disrespect of the elemental world is devastating because you do not give us the necessary protection against the ahrimanic and luciferic parasites. Many elemental beings already see that they will not get the necessary protection from humans. That is written into world karma today. There, one can see that many nature elementals will fall prey to ahrimanic and luciferic beings. The elemental kings intervened out of this concern. They hope that you humans become aware of this problem and some of you, then ever more of you, begin acting differently toward the nature elementals, until the scale of world karma begins tilting in the other direction again. Depending on how you humans act, this could go quickly.

Can I ask you another question? Why are you giving me this background information and not the elemental kings themselves?
The giant: We were of the opinion that it would convince you more if I did it. I can give you pictures out of my own experience. The elemental kings feel our concern. We wanted to enable you to experience it exactly as they do.

I notice that the conversation has ended. This was more of a lesson than a conversation. A festive and thankful mood fills my heart. Much has been given to me, and now the ball is in my court.

I look into the wide starry heavens and the vastness of the sea. A text comes to mind that is now appropriate. This has developed in the last years. The words came to me. This dedication I like speaking at the beginning of a meditation is what the giant is talking about! So I strengthen my meditative concentration, think of the elemental beings of our Earth, and speak slowly and loudly into the night wind:

> Dear elemental beings from far and near, look this way,
> Dear humans of the spheres, listen, work with us,
> Dear angel spirits, shine your light in,
> You all give strength, take light.
> We are—in the name of Christ—
> The self-creating "I",
> The sun in our hearts,
> The new Earth.

Something is still missing. The will to act. I add:

> Michael, aid us!

After a deep moment of silence, I turn back to the giant once more. He is pressing me mightily to his heart, and we say goodbye. Now I know why I had to come to Lubenicke.

The whole meeting only lasted a few minutes. I recorded it as faithfully as I could. All of the formulated words of the giant are, of course, my own. I find direct speech the best rendition in this case, because of the clear and differentiated form of communication in thought gestures and pictures that occurred between the giant and me.

⊰ **15** ⊱

Experiencing the Future Now

The meeting with the giant in Lubenicke touches me deeply, and when I wake up, I have the impression that I had been in further contact with the giant all night long. The second night I feel the same way.

I always try to make contact with the elemental world when I am awake; however, I only grasp a fraction of the exchange this way and just have a vague feeling that something is happening. When I am asleep, a lot more is happening in my subconscious, but in this case, I cannot recall what I further discussed with the giant and his elemental friends.

After the crisis intervention meeting, I had thought that the title of the book should be "Plea to Avoid Discriminating against the Elemental Beings" or "Plea to Avoid Disrespecting the Elemental Beings." Now I know these titles are not fitting and think that "Plea to Rescue the Elemental Beings" might be more appropriate. We will see.

In the afternoon, I go jogging into the interior of Cres. After a few kilometers of stony paths, an old oak tree stops me. The power of the oak permeates me from head to toe, grounds, invigorates, and enlivens me. Incredible what the energetic effect of looking at a strong oak tree can be! Even though I am already panting and sweating, I am immediately recharged and can continue running.

At that moment, the faun of the tree, a wise, old fellow, blinks at me, his glance meaning: *Great—your connection to the giant! Great—what you talked about in Lubenicke! Go on like this! This is really important!*

This faun is already informed and is encouraging me!

At the same time, a mental brake is pulled: I am jogging, and my attention is focused on the mediocre shape I am in. I am focused on the physical body and not on my body-free perceptions. I have not prepared my inner state. And so, I cannot distinguish what is projection and what is perception. I stop the braking. I can just let it be for the moment.

The faun has stopped talking. He already said what he wanted to say. I can feel him distinctly.

~~᾿ᾧᴇ ᴗᴊᴵ~~

I continue thinking about the conversation with the giant. Why was he so vague about when elemental beings will succumb to adversarial forces? It is crucial for us humans to know when the aura of the elementals will be weakened enough for ahrimanic and luciferic elementals to attack them. Will it be 100, 500, or 5,000 years from now? Certainly, there is no one fixed point in time, since this is a process and there will be a split in the nature elemental kingdom.

There will be "stronger" and "weaker" ones; some will succumb earlier, some later, and perhaps some will be able to withstand the attacks altogether. The more I think about these questions, the clearer it becomes to me that this is human logic. Elementals experience this quite differently.

The key to understanding this difference is to understand the experience of time. We earthly humans live in a time sequence. In our conceptual life, there is always a past, present, and future. The past is over for us; the future has not yet arrived. Our time perspective is strongly influenced by our age. What will happen tomorrow or next year is of great interest to us. What will be in 10 years is already less interesting. What will be in 100 years does not matter. And what will be in 1,000 years is of absolutely no concern.

The past exists in the form of memories, the future in the shape of concepts, and experiences are always in the present. I can only ever experience anything in the present moment. Even the memories of the past and the concepts of the future I can only experience in the present moment. In this sense, the past and the future are children of the present, the extended present. But we humans mostly do not have the presence of mind to take in this meaningful dimension of the present. We are sucked in by the content of the memories and do not notice their life in the present.

For elemental beings, there is no "once upon a time" or "what will be," for both are now. For elemental beings, time has the quality that space has for us: no before and after, just here and now. The future and the past are simultaneous for elemental beings, just at a different "time location." That is why elemental beings have a very different experience from us humans.

If we hear, "In 5,000 years, our city will burn down!" this leaves us cold.

On the other hand, if we hear, "Our city is burning!" we immediately take action, run into the street, and assess how far the fire is from our house. We pack up our things, get the children to safety, and help extinguish the fire. We focus all our concentration and activity on this process.

For elemental beings, there is no such difference. If they see in world karma that we will fall prey to ahrimanic and luciferic beings in 5,000 years, they experience this now and become just as active as when we hear, "Our city is on fire!" So the crisis intervention meeting and the concerned activities of the elementals are understandable in light of this.

In 2004, I did not experience this kind of flurry in the elemental world, but rather, a joyous mood full of expectation in regard to us humans. Why should the situation have changed so drastically since then that the elemental beings now fear for their existence? To the logical earthly human mind this sounds hysterical and exaggerated. But it really isn't. Elemental beings think proactively: the future in 5,000 years is just as important as the present.

The future in the spiritual world is not static but always in movement. We humans can, through our free deeds, form the future by creating karmic causes. If we lay ever more karmic causes on one side of the scale, then this side will at some point tip the scale and the "present future" in the spiritual world is created accordingly. The elementals apparently feel that humans have in the past few years placed too many karmic causes on the side of "lost to ahrimanic and luciferic beings."

The scale is now tipping in this direction, and for elemental beings this is the present reality. They suffer from this *now,* so they become active *now.* Elemental beings do not differentiate between the loss that happens tomorrow, in 100 years, or in 5,000 years.

The elemental kings have sounded the alarm at the earliest possible moment with their intervention, and that is good! For if we humans continue to place more karmic causes on the side of "decline of the elemental beings," then this side will gain more and more weight, and it will be all the harder to tip the scale in the other direction.

A second question concerns me. Elemental beings are the inside of nature forces and natural laws. If the nature elementals fall to the luciferic and ahrimanic beings, then the natural laws will also have to change in accordance with this. How can I imagine this "change" concretely? What intentions do the ahrimanic and luciferic beings have for the nature elemental beings? I make no progress with this question and let it ripen for the moment.

In hindsight, I can now clearly see what went wrong during the crisis meeting. This was obscured by my own involvement, so I could not understand the real problem the elemental beings were having and that is why I was invited to Lubenicke by the giant.

~ 16 ~

Turning Inside Out into the World

I am still preoccupied with the experiences of the last few days and want to further think things through. The elemental beings hope to work with humans, since their future depends on us. They want us to put the strength of our collective will behind them and take this future together seriously.

The elemental kings and the giant have clearly communicated to me that at present what they are most concerned about is whether our willpower is strong enough. They sincerely hope that humanity will manifest the will to act, as according to their experience, the future depends on it. At present, they are suffering as a result of our weak willpower, and this will lead to the demise of the nature elementals. It is striking that for them it is all a matter of willpower, and not what concrete measures to take. This is logical. Before every action stands the willpower needed to carry it out. A weak will results in few actions; a strong will results in many.

The concern about "will to action" the elemental beings express is similar to what underlies a marriage contract. A marriage is also a decision of will, hopefully one carried and permeated by love. You decide to stand together, even if you don't even know what that means in a concrete way. You take your partner seriously and assume responsibility. The elemental beings have proposed to humanity and are hoping that as many people as possible say yes to the marriage. The elemental beings want us to say yes—not superficially but with our whole being and heart. This is the only thing that counts.

Why are elemental beings so dependent on us? Why is it only we humans who can save them from adversarial forces? This does not seem to be a question for the elementals, because they experience it like this; however, it is a question for us humans, because we don't necessarily experience it in this way.

How can you wrap your mind around this? To give such a cosmically important role to human beings is unusual, for today, we tend to think of human beings as "errors of nature." Or perhaps you think this idea is arrogant, because only God can take on this important role. I believe that you can only understand it fully if you take our life after death into consideration. As long as you are only looking at the human being in their earthly life, the hopes expressed by the elementals are not understandable.

How have I come to know the course of life after death through my experience of the deceased and out of spiritual scientific literature?

Life after death is ideally a threefold separation, a communion with the angels, a turning inside out, and an expansion to the ends of the spiritual universe—a pulling back together of all the loose threads and a new beginning.

The first separation is when the deceased person separates from their physical body and has no more sense perceptions.

Uniting with the angels is when the angels guide and support the deceased person; without the unification with the angels the deceased stays stuck on their path.

The second separation is when the deceased person sees their whole life spread out before them—during separation from the etheric body, memories, thoughts, and feelings are spread out in front of them like a panorama.

The third separation is when the deceased person chews through their earthly life and sees and suffers through what they have done. A karma-forming self-evaluation happens, and the deceased person separates themself from their attachments. During separation from the astral body, Kamaloka, the person leaves their personality and experiences behind.

Turning inside out and expansion is when, after separating from their persona, the deceased's actual life after death begins. They turn themself inside out into the world and expand to the edges of the universe, the zodiac (Devachan). In this way they co-create world evolution, concern themself with incarnated humans, horticulture, mountain building, and so on.

Contraction is when a growing longing for the earth leads to a decision to reincarnate. In contracting, the next life is prepared together with the angels.

Taking up the loose ends again is when the cast-off astral and etheric bodies are taken up once more.

New beginning is the building of the physical body, birth into the next life.

This is of course a big subject with many questions and the subject of a separate book. Here, I want to focus on the turning inside-out into the world, because through this we humans are not separated from the world but deeply connected to it.

When I look at the starry skies, the hills, and the sea, on a specific spiritual plane I am looking at the weaving of the deceased. If the human being is not just going along for the ride but is spiritually inside the world, then it is logical that the development of humanity has an immediate effect upon the whole world and the development of the world is dependent on the human being.

This should be understandable to everyone, even if they have no concrete picture of what this "turning inside out" looks like. By thinking about it this way, we can thus comprehend the concern of the elemental beings better.

~ぐ⌒℥ん~

I want to look at this turning inside out into the world a little closer. Here I know of three possibilities:

1 *The turning inside out does not happen at all.* The deceased person got stuck through materialistic thinking or strong soul entanglements. There are countless varieties of such deceased

in ever greater quantities. They are not a constructive force for world evolution. They are not a wellspring. They do not have an abundance of power and, instead, are needy and suck energy. For the soul life of incarnated human beings, they are very problematic, nor are they helpful for nature elementals.

2 *The deceased turns themself inside out, but does not have the strength to hold their consciousness.* They sleep into the angel world, so to speak, and only wake up shortly before the next incarnation. In the meantime, they work unconsciously on world evolution and the conception of their next earthly life, but fully under the wing of the angelic hierarchies. Why do these deceased not have the strength to stay awake? I understand it in the following way: They don't have the strength, because they have not developed it in earthly life and do not bring it with them from there. Their soul life was filled only with earthly, body-based sense perceptions. These are gifted to us by the spiritual world, so they already spent their earthly life in the wake of the angelic hierarchies. This continues after death. The nature elementals are nourished by the angelic hierarchies and, therefore, also by the deceased in their wake. If the angelic hierarchies slowly pull back for the sake of human freedom, then the deceased in their wake will increasingly no longer have a connection to the nature elementals. Since they are unconscious, the deceased-in-tow can hardly act independently.

3 *The third possibility is that the deceased turns themself inside out while remaining awake.* They are working with the angels on world evolution and their next incarnation. Such deceased are wonderful. I have hardly ever experienced anything more beautiful. During my first encounters, I always thought that they were angels, because these deceased are completely filled by and identified with the angelic hierarchies and Christ. But they are more than that; they are a radiant, warm, light sun.

I experience both a boundless expansiveness and solidity, like the supporting scaffold of the cosmos. How do such deceased have the strength to stay awake? I understand the following: They bring this power from their previous lives. Their lives were not only body-based but also body-free, I-supported. The radiance of their "I," their power of concentration, their heart love holds them awake, even after turning inside out into the world. These deceased are themselves carriers, can act independently, and should be able to nourish the elemental beings even after the angels have pulled back.

In looking at these three possibilities, it becomes clear that nature elementals are especially interested in the third group, the awakened dead, for they will help carry the spiritual universe in the future. The elementals set their hopes on many radiant, awakened dead.

And Lo and Behold, I See the Light!

For the experience of the elemental beings and for staying awake after death, you need the same conditions: love, devotion, power of concentration, I-power, and body-free perception.

This solves another question: It is not immediately understandable why recognizing elemental beings spiritually holds and nourishes them. Why should the thoughts and feelings of the now incarnated human beings have such far-reaching future consequences?

I now understand the connection. The more an incarnated human being connects with the elemental world or other supersensible worlds, the more radiant power they will have as an excarnated human being. If I achieve the necessary wakefulness on Earth—not just in bodily supported perceptions but also in body-free perceptions—then I will have this wakefulness at my disposal after death.

The more recognition the elementals receive on Earth, the more awakened dead there will be, able to carry the elemental beings! Only with this insight can I understand the insistent plea of the giant in Lubenicke. The giant said: "If you respect us and permeate us with consciousness and love, then you give us the support and strength to carry on. You illuminate, glow through us, and spiritualize us. Through this, you are also reconnecting us with the angelic world. For the angels live in human freedom. The angels live in the light of your consciousness." The illumination of the elemental beings does not just happen now, but unfolds properly and permanently after death, if the dead stay awake.

Why am I struggling so much to understand and decode all this? Couldn't I simply ask the elemental beings? This would be of little use, because they have already transmitted what they can transmit. If I continue asking, this would not be helpful. If there were new answers at all, I would in turn need to understand these. There is no way around grasping the relationships independently using your mind. In my eyes, it is not possible to lean back in an armchair and let the spiritual world serve you, for spirit beings can only transmit that for which the receiver has receptive organs. Such organs of understanding are formed though the mental grasp of spiritual relationships.

How can you imagine in a palpable way the deceased turning themselves inside out, staying awake, and so becoming the nourishing ground for the elemental beings?

A few days after I met Angar, in the summer of 2005, I could experience all of this in a very practical and touching way. The natural wonder of the Plitvicer Lakes in Croatia is a many-tiered lake landscape full of waterfalls and fountains. This landscape was built as a result of stones building up. A type of algae makes the stones grow. It is, however, unclear why this is happening in such a concentrated way at this particular spot in the river and not as strongly at other places along the riverbed. There must be something special here.

Agnes and I marveled at this wonder for two days. I found several bigger water beings, connected myself to them through my heart, and asked their origin. Every time and repeatedly, I was taken by the water beings into the mood of a pious, pure, praying human community and to a magnificent turned-inside-out deceased human being. I was not led to an angel when I asked the nature elemental what its origin was, as I usually am.

Slowly it became clearer.

Five hundred years ago, there was a small, modest, monastic community in the region of the Plitvicer Lakes. In the center stood a holy woman. The secret of this community was the intimacy and bliss of her meditative prayer. The elemental beings of the landscape were permeated by the substance she created through her prayers.

The community was concerned with the question of how to maintain its religious powers in the future—its powers were generated during life, and after death they would unfold. The holy woman's intimate prayer developed into new ground for elemental beings; they no longer stood on angelic beings but on the dead spirits of this praying community. I could experience a deceased soul looking lovingly and powerfully out of the cosmic periphery at the Plitvicer Lakes and carrying these elemental beings.

The question about how to maintain the community's religious powers led to the stones growing and the creation of this wonder of the natural world—the local elementals took up the desire to do this from the deceased souls (strongly supported by the angels, of course), and the elemental beings put it into practice, causing the stones to grow. To serve as fertile ground, humans need not know the details—that is the job of the elementals and the angels—but must deliver the will, the idea, and the spiritual connection.

Every year, hundreds of thousands of visitors, many carrying video equipment and cameras, are touched in their souls by this holy place. If you want to feel God, I recommend a visit to the Plitvicer Lakes.

As a result of my Plitvicer Lake experience, I now pay attention to this aspect in my meetings with the elementals, and I continue to meet elemental beings who either already stand on or want to stand on a human foundation.

For example, a group of dwarves in the Forum 3 cultural center in Stuttgart comes to mind. They were suffering from being cut off from the angelic world and not having found real human ground to stand on yet, and so were hanging in the air. I experienced a kind of digesting in me, and the dwarves becoming more satisfied. As a result of my perceiving them and shining the light of my attention and heart warmth on them, they received new ground on which they could stand. I reckon I will stay connected to this group of dwarves for a long time.

In spiritually oriented places, conference centers, biodynamic farms, and so forth, I often find elemental beings permeated by humans. The people involved don't necessarily have to experience this consciously; just loving, open attention is enough.

Elementals that stand on a human foundation often have a strong connection to the time spirit Michael and receive his powers. In this sense, you could speak of Michaelic elemental beings. I understand that if we humans become the free carriers of the earth, then we have Michael standing behind us, who offers us his strength.

I don't know how many elementals reside on human ground. There are many regions where I experience nothing of the sort. Is this because of the region or because of my limited powers of perception and scanty impressions? To come to a well-founded conclusion about this would be the task of a research project that should be divided up among several people. The elemental kings and the giants of Lubenicke seem to think that the percentage is much too low.

~\ 17 /~

Everyday Working Together

The crisis meeting and the conversation with the giant were about the big picture. How can I now break this down? What experiences have I had with the daily interactions of humans and elemental beings?

Connecting to a Place

The soul connection with a place or house is a connection with the elemental beings. For instance, when I come into my office, I am greeted by the elemental beings there and I feel at home. Having been born in the Allgäu, I have the experience of being welcomed by the regional elemental beings every time I go there. They stream into my aura and heart. I usually cannot distinguish separate elemental beings; it is an overall impression.

In order to really arrive at a place, I like to look for a big, leading elemental being, an earth master or Pan. In connecting with them I connect to the place. If I do not do this, it takes days for me to feel at home.

Imprinting Places

Even if we are not conscious of it, we continually imprint elemental beings on places and spaces. This always strikes me when I enter an apartment I've never been to before. How different the atmosphere can be, a perfect match to the people who live there! This fit is due to the imprint made by the human inhabitants on the elementals of the apartment, attracting new ones or chasing old ones away.

I have often noticed that the mood is not dependent on the décor. You can find the picture-perfect type of spaces, perfectly arranged with flowers and an open book on the table, yet with a general mood of emptiness and forlornness. Superficial décor is not enough to create a dense elemental population; the space needs to have heart.

Also striking to me are the elemental beings found in places of work. A judicial building, a department store, a bakery, a locksmith's shop, or a farm may reflect a huge range of different moods. It's clear that specific tasks breed corresponding types of elemental beings over the years.

The imprint of a place is reciprocal. In a carpentry workshop, dwarves help with the sawing and hammering. At the university, math elementals help the students with arithmetic. The imprint of places has been impressively researched by biologist Rupert Sheldrake, who writes about morphogenetic fields.[3]

Greeting

For me, the secret key to the elemental world is established by greeting. It bothered me for a long time that I could not bring myself to perceive the elementals regularly. Then I noticed that I do not think of the elementals every day, let alone greet them. If I am not even doing that, paying that much attention to them, why should I be able to perceive them?

So I began with a daily greeting meditation, and did this for a few months. I formed concrete concepts for earth, water, fire,

---

[3] Rupert Sheldrake, *Das schöpferische Universum. Die Theorie des morphogenetischen Feldes,* Berlin: Ullstein Verlag, 1993. English edition: Rupert Sheldrake, *Morphic Resonance: The Nature of Formative Causation.* Rochester: Park Street Press, 2009.

air, and Christ elemental beings until a feeling arose and then greeted these separate groups. I paid a lot of attention to having the greeting really come from the heart.

For me this has had a great effect, as it has allowed me to build the bridges into the elemental world I had been fruitlessly seeking while simultaneously clearing blocking beliefs. Greeting the elementals in a heartfelt way every day has allowed many hidden doubts, disbeliefs, dissatisfactions in various guises to come to the surface from the depths of my soul, and I was able to free myself of these emotional and mental blockages.

Thanking, Speaking, Feeding, Cleaning

I created a meditation exercise out of this greeting. It can be very simple. One thought a day brings about miracles:

Dear apartment beings, how are you? I will be gone for two days. Take good care of yourselves.

I will soon be going to sleep. Dear elemental beings of the landscape, let me in.

Anyone who speaks to the elementals regularly and naturally, says thank you on occasion, and takes them in by saying grace before meals is doing a lot. The elementals experience all of it. And definitely your feeling for where you live, the garden, the part of town you're in will change, as the elementals work through these subtle changes in sensitivity. This is already communicating with the elementals. It does not have to be an intricate story like the one I recount in this book.

A very nice custom is the feeding of elemental beings. For instance, you give them a little bit of your lunch on a little plate. This is a wonderful way of saying thank you and including them in your life!

You can turn uncomfortable activities into fun ones if you invite the elementals:

Dear apartment being, help me vacuum. Not only is there dust but also a lot of astral garbage that should be disposed of.

Dear undines, how playfully the water washes the dirt from the dishes! Would you like to wash with me?

Illumination

I have often asked myself how it is for elemental beings to receive attention from humans? I think for them it is similar to how we humans experience the sunrise—it gets light, we are warmed, and all of life changes. How would the days unfold if the sun were to no longer rise?

I experience my attention as an etheric current carrying the spiritual light of the "I" as well as the light of the angel connected to this "I." You cannot look at an elemental being from the outside, as you can with sense objects; you can only permeate elemental beings, become one with them, and the elemental being is then a different one from before. It has received a new substance. It has received the luminous power of attention and the warmth of the human heart.

Elemental beings are illuminated even if the person cannot grasp their experiences subtly enough to clearly know they are dealing with an elemental. For us humans, the difference between conceiving of and believing in the elementals and clearly perceiving them is huge.

For the elementals, though, the difference is minor; for them, it is more important to receive heart vibrations and the power of attention. That is their sunrise.

Elemental Being First Aid

Time and again, I meet elemental beings in need of help. One of my first conscious meetings with a nature elemental being was a big earth being in Kempten-Lenzfried. On my walks, I always experienced unpleasant, cloying feelings beside an old red beech tree next to the golf course. Twenty meters in front and behind this spot I didn't have these feelings. There was no external explanation.

I experienced this for a year and paid no more attention to it. Then, while participating in a geomancy seminar, I received specific guidance, and the next time I took a walk wanted to take a closer look.

I went into the usual bad mood while watching my soul state and found an ancient, crippled earth being, about five meters wide. It appeared to be holding its tummy and bending over in pain. Apparently, this earth being was asking me for help and had tried to capture my attention for a long time. I was still very inexperienced at the time, but I knew it needed heart strength and to solve its problem, so it would be good to find the cause.

I meditated on the earth being for about half an hour and tried to systematically shine my heart into every corner of its soul realm. This felt like excavation, a loosening of something solid. Slowly, I became aware that stuck fears, mortal fears were blocking the earth elemental. I had a sudden realization: during the Napoleonic era, there had been a battle on this ground that left a few dozen dead. There was even a gravestone commemorating this under the beech tree.

When this connection became clear to me, I had the feeling that my heart was truly penetrating the soul space of the earth being. I kept looking at it in my imagination and was very surprised. In front of me stood a young, upright fellow, brimming with strength! This is how he is still standing, taking care of the meadows and hills.

In a small park in Bochum, I once found a desperate faun above a tree that had fallen down. He had obviously not realized that his tree was now lying on the ground or was taken by surprise when the tree suddenly fell during a storm. He was now hanging in the air in a desperate way, did not know which way was up, and had become emotionally stuck. In this case, all it took was heartfelt compassion, a bit of coaxing, and calming and the faun could leave his former place and task. The next day I went back for a second look, and he was gone. Surely, a Pan had helped him find a new tree.

On a farm near Rosenberg, I contacted a leading earth being that has its focus in the entrance there. This earth being had a beautiful golden radiance. It approached me joyfully and told me that it knew me. I asked, how so?

It was present during a meditation I had led in Dornach near Basel, when we had greeted the elemental beings. When we greet in this way, I always have the feeling that many elementals are taking part, but I cannot distinguish between them. Apparently, word gets out and elemental beings even come from far away. This is no problem for them, since elemental beings do not live in space.

The earth being changed the subject right away and had a strong request. I should immediately go to the manure pits behind the stable as there was something I had to do there!

Between the manure pits, I found a water being that was clearly in bad shape. Emaciated and listless, it looked at me sadly on a soul level. I expressed my concern, gave it strength, and felt myself through the being. It became clear that it had become blocked by the quarreling and ensuing social tension on the farm a few years ago.

Offering compassion and finding out what the problem was was enough to solve it. The water being cheered up, and I saw it jumping into the manure pit and diving deep down. Later, it became apparent that the problem was not entirely solved. The water being was still unhappy, because manure pits are the life sphere of fire beings. The water being was focused in the wrong spot, so it was placed in a more fitting location.

In Leipzig, I stepped into a small back courtyard and found a big water being there. The owner of the house told me she had been having problems with water and humidity in the cellar for a long time. Two geomancers found a wedged-in water being under the ceiling of the cellar. This being had come into this uncomfortable position through earlier construction work.

The geomancers relocated the water being to the courtyard in order to free it, but this didn't work right away and had to be tried several times. To make the water being feel more at home, they installed a little gurgling water basin. After this the water problems stopped in the cellar, the landlady told me.

So it is possible for nature elementals to become wedged in on the soul level or traumatized. They can then no longer work properly and get stuck. This may happen when nature elementals are confronted with strong human emotions, such as the fear of death of dying soldiers or grueling family disputes. Also, construction work that has not taken the elementals into consideration can lead to problems.

I understand that human interventions can lead to blockages. How this is also possible through a natural occurrence like the fallen tree is still a mystery to me. The rescue service for elemental beings is an important mission for us humans to fulfill. The elementals also have a human rescue service. Some bigger elemental beings have the exclusive task of disposing of human soul waste and encrusted thought forms.

Psychotherapy with Elementals

I believe that the rediscovery of elementals can be a big help for psychotherapy. Modern psychotherapy often describes the human personality as a flock of elementals, but uses other words like "soul aspects" or "inner family." Some types of therapy, such as

Psychodynamic Imaginative Trauma Therapy (PITT) developed by Luise Reddemann or Katathym Imaginative Psychotherapy (KIP) work directly with the elementals. Knowing about the elemental beings would make this more understandable and offer a conceptual grounding.

A central problem of soul illnesses is that the patient identifies with their illness. If we were to always address the pathological fear as a fear elemental, it would be easier for the patient to bring the fear in front of them, speak to it as an independent being, and help transform it. Just the thought that the human personality is a conglomerate of elementals is already healing, since it creates a free space for the human "I."

↲ 18 ↳

Collaboration during
the Referendum

As I reflect on the concrete achievements that are possible when we work with elemental beings, Hamburg comes to mind, where the first opportunity to work with the elementals for socio-political change presented itself in 2004.

On June 13, 2004, Hamburg wrote a piece of democratic history: the referendum for Fair Voting Rights was approved by 256,507 Hamburg residents, representing 66.5 percent of the population. For the first time in German history, citizens themselves would be able to decide how members of parliament should be voted into office. It was a massive win for sovereignty!

Every campaign must accomplish the following tasks: a clearly stated argument, organization, media, finances, campaign literature, keeping volunteers motivated, and so on. In my eyes, one more task should be added to this list: cooperation with the elemental and angelic worlds.

In Hamburg, more than anywhere else in Germany, political parties consolidated power through favorable election laws—voters were only allowed to cast a single vote on a set list of statewide candidates for each party, and the parties determined who would sit in parliament according to the order of listed candidates. This meant that parliamentary representatives voted along party lines and adhered 100 percent to the party whip rather than represent the views of the electorate. As a result, the political landscape had become unrepresentative and alienated voters.

The successful Fair Voting Rights referendum led to the introduction of voting districts, so depending on the size of the district, three to five direct candidates could be voted into office. As for the lists of candidates, the voters now got several votes and could get behind individual candidates on these lists, thereby accumulating and splitting the vote and making the representatives more independent of party affiliation.

The petition for the referendum was started by More Voter Rights, More Democracy, The Omnibus for More Democracy, and other citizen initiatives. This success was not the end of the story, though. The ruling CDU (conservative party) did everything it could to reverse the referendum, and for many years, the struggle for fair voting rights and direct democracy continued in Hamburg.

Angels Working in Society

Every human being is escorted by a guardian angel that stands behind them and supports and strengthens them. There are also angels connected to groups of people, the archangels. The time spirits, or archai, carry the impulses of a whole epoch for all of humanity.

I had long been interested in the question of how angels work in society. In the beginning, my interest was theoretical but became increasingly practical. I practiced connecting with my soul so that I could let myself be guided by the will of the angels. This became an indispensable source of strength and inspiration.

From 1992 to 1995, I was responsible for organizing the petition for the More Democracy in Bavaria referendum, which aimed to introduce referendum rights to all Bavarian municipalities and cities. During several intense months of inner processing regarding this project, I repeatedly witnessed in meditation the referendum transforming into a multitude of angels sounding trumpets beautifully and powerfully from the heavens. This experience was accompanied by a strong feeling of evidence and seemed more real than the material world. It gave me the assurance that the project was supported by the angels.

This deep experience obligated me to fully commit to the success of the petition for the referendum, and I literally gave this task my all. In the years that followed, this angel experience was an important touchstone for my soul, and it nourished me and was my greatest source of motivation.

Michael's Patronage

I thought that the Hamburg petition for the Fair Voting Rights referendum could also only be successful if it were supported by the spiritual world. I always carried this in my consciousness and asked for help. The goals, honest motivation, and heartfelt commitment of the circle of people petitioning for the Hamburg referendum convinced me that it had the support of the angelic world.

Evidence if this in the real world eventually came after two years of work on this project, at the beginning of the registration period, in September 2003. The petition for a referendum needed to be signed by 70,000 registered voters in order for the referendum to take place. Here is my firsthand account:

On the first day of the two-week period allotted to collecting these signatures, a spirit touches me as I sit meditating on the referendum; one could say it breezes through me. I recognize him; it is the time spirit Michael. Michael is the angel that concerns himself with the freedom of the human being. In my experience, he only takes up direct contact with a human being if you approach him and lift yourself up to him when there is really something at stake. To me, Michael is a countenance behind which higher beings stand who are not directly visible but who radiate through him. This is a very short encounter; nevertheless, it is accompanied by an experience of evidence. With his appearance, his name is expressed at the same time. He has a special power and a distinctive coloring that is unshakable, since it consists of itself. He guides the world in an impersonal way. His message is that the petition for the referendum is under his protection, and that it can therefore be successful and will be successful—if we humans do our part. We are, of course, all very nervous, wondering if we can collect the necessary 70,000 signatures in the next 14 days?

This was successful! In the course of the two weeks, people become more open and friendly, ever more ready to offer their signature. Most significantly, the weather is on our side. We have continual sunshine, in spite of being in Hamburg! It rains only on the last day of the registration period. At this point we already have close to 80,000 signatures. The rain then continues for a long time. If it had begun a week earlier, our results would have plummeted and we would surely have lost the petition for the referendum. You cannot collect signatures in the rain; people are in a bad mood and much more difficult to approach than during friendly sunshine, so we were protected by a good spirit!

Pan and the Water Being

In the time between the petition for the referendum in September 2003 and the referendum in June 2004, I found new portals to the elemental and spiritual worlds, and as a result, I grew more determined to actively seek cooperation with these worlds. Just as I made phone calls to recruit volunteers to distribute flyers, I also wanted to concern myself with the cooperation of the elemental world.

How to do this, though? I was still very inexperienced, but it felt right to talk to the elementals and angels about the petition for the referendum and ask for their assistance.

I spent Pentecost 2004 with Agnes in a park that is an old cemetery in Hamburg Altona. Here, there was a big, significant tree that had been chosen as a focal point by a Pan, a leading elemental being responsible for the tree and plant life of a greater region. If I connected meditatively with this tree, I not only experienced the tree but was connected to a larger region, so I approached this Pan with my request.

This was, of course, not easy. For one thing, I needed to find a good connection to the Pan and make my request understandable, and I could not say it in words, because elemental beings do not understand words, only feelings and the meaning underlying the words. So I tried to nonverbally communicate the intention of the petition for the referendum and to ask for energetic support. After about an hour of trying I took a break, with the feeling of not being finished yet.

On the second try, I experienced the Pan more clearly and could voice my request openly. I witnessed an energy sinking like a protective mantel around and into the Pan. That was Michael, who was giving Pan protection and support for this task. Satisfied, I ended the meditation. I now knew that the referendum would also receive the support of Michael!

The question came up as to why I needed to talk to the Pan before Michael got involved? Why didn't he instruct Pan directly? He apparently waits for a request, a move from the human toward him, before he becomes active. The angelic world leaves the human being completely free and waits patiently before helping.

In the afternoon, we were outside Hamburg, near Elmshorn. By chance, I met a big water being near the River Krückau. I was astonished by the ease with which I could make contact, and I tried to connect this water being energetically to the Pan. I suggested to the water being that it could inform the water beings of Hamburg of the coming referendum.

On the River Elbe, Agnes and I perceived a stream of warmth flowing toward Hamburg. The Elbe is Hamburg's gateway to the world—above the water, and against the direction of flow, etheric warmth and lightness blew toward Hamburg.

I was not sure what more I could do, so I asked Wolfgang Schneider, an experienced geomancer who knows Hamburg. He made it clear to me that you can unconsciously force elemental beings and bind them to the task; you should put the request in such a way as to leave them free, so they can decide for themselves what they want to do. He also suggested that I visit a leading earth being and a leading water being in Hamburg, but I no longer had time for this, since I was leaving Hamburg to go to Wangen in the Allgäu for a Beuys symposium, where I was to give a seminar.

Joseph Beuys Takes Part

Joseph Beuys (1921–1986) is considered by art historians to be the most significant German artist in the second half of the 20th century. He expanded the concept of art, relating it to society and the human world. To build what he called the "social sculpture," the right of referendum is essential, allowing each person to participate equally.

Joseph Beuys founded the Organization for Direct Democracy Through Referendum, with an office in Düsseldorf in 1971. In 1972, he installed the office at the international art exhibit *documenta 5* in Kassel and spoke for 100 days to visitors about the expanded concept of art and direct democracy. Joseph Beuys was thus one of the most important promoters of the referendum concept, and a source of inspiration for many people who are still actively involved with direct democracy.

Beuys conventions took place at irregular intervals. On October 1, 1995, the day of the successful More Democracy in Bavaria referendum, there was a Beuys symposium in Kranen-burg. On September 27, 1998, there was a Beuys convention in Kassel while the vote for the More Democracy in Hamburg referendum was taking place. The Beuys convention in Bochum took place in the middle of the successful petition for the More Democracy in Thüringen referendum, which was signed by almost 400,000 people in the course of four months. The 2003 Beuys symposium took place at the beginning of the six-month-long petition for the More Democracy in South Tirol

Referendum. And the 2004 Beuys symposium was now only a week before the Fair Voting Rights in Hamburg referedum.

On the one hand, several hundred people got together to create new artistic and social impulses in the spirit of Joseph Beuys. Through this, Beuys got a special stream of attention from us humans. On the other hand, big events were happening in society in which the people themselves were fighting for direct democracy.

Direct democracy was not introduced or improved by the parliaments but by the people themselves. In 1995, 1998, and 2004, the Beuys conventions took place during the actual referendums, not during the preceding petition for referendum period. In Thüringen, it stopped with the petition for the referendum; the referendum was forbidden by law, but parliament still put a lot of the demands into practice. The decisive process was thus the petition for the referendum in the fall of 2000. Also, in south Tirol, the petition phase was the decisive phase for the formation of the will of the people, since the law forbids referendums.

In light of these astonishing timings, one strongly gets the impression that Joseph Beuys is helping with these processes of self-empowerment of the people through direct democracy. My impression is confirmed. Beginning with the Beuys symposium in 2004 and ending with the referendum on June 13, 2004, I experience how Beuys is following this process attentively. I experience him spread out over the whole world, looking on from the wide periphery of the physical world, and thereby giving support and encouragement to the process of the referendum.

In order to come to this perception of Beuys, I look at the physical world in a panoramic way and inwardly tune into the realm of the deceased, then specifically to Beuys himself. This works because Beuys, being dead, is no longer active in the soul realm but lives purified in the spiritual universe; he has lifted himself up to become the "inside" of the physical world, which he forms together with other deceased people.

Hamburg Is Etherically Activated

On June 7, I took the train to Hamburg again and was curious to see what awaited me in the week prior to the referendum vote on June 13. I used the train ride for a longer meditation. Surprisingly, I experienced clearly the whole of Hamburg on an elemental level. It literally came toward me. It is not enough to concentrate on a spiritual being or a theme; rather, this being or theme must come toward you in order for you to experience it intensely. In the spiritual realm, you cannot perceive something "on command," only through your own will; the spiritual world must have an active interest in you having the perception.

I experienced the elemental region of Hamburg as filled with light, warm beings descending from heaven. At first, I believed them to be angels, but they turned out to be elemental beings resembling angels with accompanying ether forces. This was a light and joyous event! In order to exclude any error, I tried to look at other cities in a similar way. They looked different, more distant in my perception, and not so impressive. So the elemental region I was experiencing was really Hamburg. What was happening here on a subtler level?

The following morning, June 8, I was overwhelmed by Hamburg! The sun was shining, and I walked through the streets in a state of wonder and experienced everything filled with happy, friendly, warm ether forces. I had never experienced anything like it! These ether forces had a special character. They felt more objective, purer than other ether forces. Everything was full. I felt like I was walking through clouds, and I was particularly surprised by my experience of this energy as being imprinted with helpful information for the referendum.

I could hardly believe it! Did the spiritual world fill a whole city with well-meaning ether forces in order to support a referendum? Was this really true, or was I beginning to hallucinate?

I was on a bus at the Holstenstrasse train station, where there was a medium-sized fire being with which I have often had an easy contact. While riding past, I asked it if it was really true that the spiritual world was charging Hamburg etherically? The fire being winked at me and said, yes, this was true. But it hardly had time to answer since it was busy dispensing these ether forces and had its hands full.

In Altona, where the bus promoting direct democracy was stationed, Regine, a co-worker, told me that she was looking for sunglasses in order to view the Venus eclipse. This gave me further insight. Today, from 7:20 a.m. to 1:20 p.m., the planet Venus was making the transit between the earth and the sun, a rare occurrence that only happens once every 130 years. Venus energy was joining forces with sun energy, so the etheric activation was evidently part of a larger planetary scheme.

The Stubborn Earth Master

During the day I distributed pamphlets. I was happy to be outside and able to connect with the city. In the afternoon I went to the Michel, the church above the port that is a Hamburg landmark. I wanted to visit the earth elemental being that had its focus there, following Wolfgang Schneider's recommendation. I went around the church and found the elemental quickly.

A further surprise! I had never met such a huge earth being. It was almost as big as the church! The first, more external perception proved easy, but it was more difficult to go farther into it. After a half hour of meditation, I was successful. I tried to greet the elemental being and tell it of my concern, but this was not really successful.

The earth being took over the conversation and showed me that it was ancient, several thousand years old. When it came into being, Hamburg did not exist yet, and there was no land here, only ocean. I asked when it was born and according to the sensations and pictures the earth being showed me, I had the feeling that it came into being during Atlantean times. I asked how it came into being. It showed me two angel-like beings flying next to each other over the waters. Both turned toward the water and circled toward each other. At the moment they flew past each other, the earth being was created, but it was still very small—it had gained its present volume over the course of centuries.

Now I experienced the expansion of the earth being even more. It was enormous; I felt like a fly sitting on an elephant. The influence of this earth master reached beyond Hamburg.

I now tried to get back to my concern: the referendum.

But the earth master was not interested and said (of course not in words): *I am ancient and huge and have been managing the earth masses for centuries. So what do you want: voting rights? What kind of human stuff is that? Voting rights? I am not concerned with such trivialities. I am an earth master, and ancient.*

Of course, why would an elemental being be concerned with a referendum and voting rights? These are human concepts and do not fit into the life sphere of an elemental being.

I made another effort. I asked the earth master to look at the deeper impulse behind the referendum: it was a step on the human path to becoming a free being; Christ was at the center of the referendum. I gave it my best shot, thinking with the tongues of angels, but I did not reach the earth master.

I was about to give up, when things took a surprising turn. The substance of the earth master was permeated by an energy well known to me. I experienced Michael pervading the earth master and communicating that the voting rights referendum was under his own protection, because it was in line with advancing earth development. Michael then pulled back again.

Finally, I was able to talk to the earth master. As if nothing had happened, it received my concern, but when it came to how it could support me, it balked again. It was the manager of the earth elementals. What was it to do for a referendum? I tried to encourage it by saying that it was big and influential and certainly would have ideas, but it remained stubborn, saying that it was an earth elemental and did not understand anything about referendums.

It became clear to me that I needed to give the earth master a stronger push. It could suggest to all earth beings of Hamburg that they give humans a nudge. This could be mentally, through a feeling, or by guiding their glance toward a billboard, for instance. There were many possibilities. What the humans then did with this was their concern and responsibility, but a nudge would be permissible and helpful. The earth master ended up sharing my point of view.

The Purification

The next morning, a huge storm awoke us, thundering, storming, and raining buckets. All of a sudden it became pitch black. Had someone switched off the sun? Was the world coming to an end? I looked out the window. Hard to believe, but a pitch-black cloud passed by. I had never seen such a dark cloud. The newspapers later reported that the "monster thunderstorm" uprooted 2,000 trees. It was as though witches had covered Hamburg in a black cloud. Had the etheric activation of Hamburg involving the Venus energy and the cooperation of the elementals led to a release of old thinking and feeling patterns blocking Hamburg's collective soul space, thereby purifying it of elemental witches?

The Elemental World Pleads for Help

I was worried: Did I now have to speak with every elemental being as I had done with the earth master? Did each one need to be asked separately? I assumed elemental beings form a unity and are interconnected, so that it is enough to come into contact with one of them. But the earth master had required special attention. Who else needed this? Today was Wednesday, the referendum was on Sunday, and such encounters are very exhausting for me, I could not do it for more than two or three hours a day.

After my daily distribution of pamphlets, I went down to the River Elbe to visit with a Neptune, a leading water elemental responsible for the inner region of the city of Hamburg. This encounter allayed my concern. After a longer preparation, I tried to tell it of the purpose of the referendum, but it was already well informed and had been working for the referendum for a while already. I had already talked to its colleague on the Krückau . . . I asked how it was actively working for the referendum. It told me that as a water being, it washed souls and carried away doubts and fears that were sitting like thorns in human souls regarding the referendum.

I asked the Neptune if there were still elementals in Hamburg that were not participating and needed help. It led me to a big fire being that was very frustrated and embittered. I asked where it had its focus. I felt it coming from the direction of the southwest but could not quite make it out exactly, so I went through several parts of the city and got a positive resonance with Wilhelmsburg.

I felt into the fire being and opened myself to its sorrow. It was totally frustrated by the egotism and aggression of the humans it was dealing with. I took on its sorrow and tried to offer comfort, explaining that egotism is an obstacle for humans so that they can grow. In overcoming egotism, the human becomes a being of freedom, and this is the goal of earth evolution and, therefore, egotism is a necessary, if bitter, in-between step. I got the impression that the fire being's concerns were somewhat assuaged by my empathy.

This was a clear meeting over distance. In the elemental world you can go anywhere in thoughts. Later, I find out that Wilhelmsburg is not in the southwest but in the south. My sense of direction and my inner question regarding the location did not correspond. I cannot clear up this discrepancy.

Afterwards I connected with a big air being and had the impression that everything was alright and no further communication was necessary.

How did things develop with the earth master?

I returned to the Michel church. Everything seemed fine with the earth master. It was friendly. I asked the earth master if it knew of other elementals not yet engaged with the referendum in need of a helpful nudge? It drew my attention across the street in the direction of a group of trees.

How far should I go? It was apparently quite nearby. I crossed the street. It should be on this playground. Oh, dear! I found a suffering, wounded, middle-sized earth being that appeared incapacitated. I tried to make contact with it and found its heart bound by a black substance making it unable to function. It quickly became clear to me that this was a bondage situation that had been consciously brought about by humans and would not be a simple case. I cut it short and postponed until tomorrow.

Power Meditation for the Referendum

That evening we visited a channeling session. A medium purported to channel the archangel Michael. I had never attended a channeling session and wanted to get my own impression. There were over 200 people in the hall, almost exclusively women. As a warm-up there was a conversation. I asked for Michael's support for the referendum. The medium took this up and suggested a group meditation.

After the break, more than 200 people meditated on the success of the referendum for several minutes. This was a very strong, dignified moment that reached out far beyond the hall. Other participants later confirmed that this was the strongest moment of the whole evening. The power of group meditation and prayer in political action once again became clear to me through this experience! This is one of the most powerful means at our disposal.

One more remark about this channeling session, since Michael was already mentioned previously in this book. After long processing and feeling through the events of this evening, I came to the conclusion that the medium was not channeling the archangel Michael but a deceased guru or healer who did not want to merge with world consciousness after death but wanted to hold himself in his own domain. He fed off the forces of devotion brought to him by the channelings. The deceased person claimed he was Michael, for this gave him a bigger audience. Since I had strongly connected with the channeling, I could now experience how this deceased person had tried to ensconce himself in the back of my aura and I then had to, with some effort, lovingly rid myself of him again. Of course, many channelings are real. This is dependent on the constitution and protective measures of the medium.

Struggle with a Black Magician

The next day, Thursday, June 10, 2004, I returned to the playground near the Michel church in order to devote myself to the wounded earth being. I had two contradictory feelings. On the one hand, I was worried about the task at hand; on the other hand, I felt an obligation to the earth master.

Why on earth had it given me this task? Apparently, it could not do anything itself here and thought I could solve the situation on its behalf. I was not so sure, but I did not want to disappoint the earth master, and I also felt sorry for the wounded earth being.

I found it in the same condition as yesterday. It was suffering and bent over and bound with a black substance in its heart.

I did not know what I was dealing with, so I asked the earth being what had happened and why.

With a tearful voice, it responded that it didn't know why it was bewitched. A tragic random blow of destiny had struck because it was connected to this place.

I concentrated on this black and very unpleasant substance and struggled with it for a long time, but it was spiritually impermeable.

I know of dreadful ahrimanic beings that work with luciferic beings and form the foundation of human egotism. If you permeate these ahrimanic beings with love, you can free them, and they are quite happy about this, for they have provided the resistance and sacrificed themselves for humans in order to develop themselves into cosmically free beings. The black substance was somehow connected to this, but also quite different. You can permeate ahrimanic beings spiritually, but here I found no entrypoint. It was the densest spiritual matter I had ever encountered. This might sound strange, because this black substance was materially not even visible; it was "spiritual matter." Every visible stone is like air in comparison!

Slowly, it dawned on me what I had to do. I was not dealing with normal evil here but with potentized evil, with conscious evil. The evil of egotism normally works out of the subconscious and is therefore not really evil, because there was never a conscious human decision toward evil. But here I was dealing with the result of a conscious human decision to do evil.

For the first time, I experienced what this brings about: impermeable, forever bound, black, death-bringing dross. In the nadir of our being, cut off from the universe, we humans have the freedom to "enlighten" matter or to further densify it. I now understood what Rudolf Steiner means when he speaks of an "incorrigible moon" separating the end of Earth evolution as the earth becomes completely spiritual. Here, I was already dealing with a piece of this "incorrigible moon."

But was it really true that this substance could not be spiritually transformed? I tried again to summon all my heart forces to meet this substance, but there was nothing to be done. Perhaps something can still be pressed out in the future. It will become one of our greatest future tasks to press out such black clots in order for the "incorrigible moon" to become as small as possible, but I made no progress here.

Who on earth had created this stuff? Where did it come from? I concentrated on the origin and could see a black energy line coming out of the substance and evidently leading to the creator. I tried to follow this line of energy but was not successful. How could I help the earth being? Even if I could not transform this stuff, perhaps I could separate it from the earth being?

I tried to mentally separate the substance from the earth being. Since I did not know how to do this, I called on the angels for help and, lo and behold, I soon experienced angelic energy surrounding the black substance and packing it in to make it free floating and transportable. So far so good, but where should I now send the stuff? I could not burden anyone else with it, so where should it go?

Suddenly, I was confronted with a Gorleben final repository problem (Gorleben is a "temporary" storage place for atomic waste in Germany). Why was I even burdening myself with it? The black magician should get his black stuff back! And so, I sent the substance wrapped in the angelic light in the direction of the magician. This was not easy, because I still felt it as being trapped in the earth being. I concentrated on the process.

At that moment, a middle-aged woman with a backpack appeared in the playground and sat down on a bench about three meters from me. She was clearly a homeless drug addict. Her face was haggard and deformed by a rash. About 15 safety pins were stuck through each of her ears.

Instantly, she snapped at me with a loud and aggressive voice. I should immediately "stop thinking!" I was an "asshole," and "the shit is still clinging to your face," and so on.

I nodded in a friendly way, moved a few meters away, and tried to concentrate on transporting my substance again. Immediately, the woman started bellowing again, I should stop "thinking." And if I do not do this instantly, I would get an "injection in my behind." She is a drug addict and knows how to do this. And she goes on in this way. I understood that I could not continue to work, said goodbye, and left the place.

Now I had the trouble on my hands I had been afraid of! This black magician had, of course, immediately understood that I was trying to free the elemental being of his stuff. Carelessly, I had even sent his stuff back to him, so he induced this woman to come and yell at me that I should "stop thinking!" I had never been yelled at for this reason before. Usually, people could not care less whether I am thinking or not. How did the black magician provoke this woman to make her appearance? I had no idea how this worked. He was obviously clairvoyant to immediately notice my interventions. I went home exhausted.

The next day, Friday, June 11, 2004, I again visited the elemental being after distributing pamphlets. My work yesterday remained incomplete, and I was dissatisfied. I noticed that the elemental being was indeed not completely free yet. The black stuff had been loosened, but was not completely gone. I again organized a transport and sent well-meaning, de-escalating thoughts in the direction of the black magician: I only want to free the elemental being . . . I promised someone, and if I promise something, I have to do it . . . I am not at all interested in him . . . He should do what he wants . . .

I did not want to draw attention to myself and made it a quick action. This time, I was not disturbed. I had the impression that the transport was complete.

Why was I spending so much time with this black stuff? Was this really important for the referendum? Whether the earth being was capable of action or not could not be decisive because it was not a very big being. Perhaps it got the sympathy of other elemental beings in Hamburg which realized that they would get help from humans in the face of threats they could not handle.

In any case, it was the bidding of the earth master, and if I did not take this seriously, it would notice and there would be consequences.

The next day, I noticed that I was still open to the black magician in my aura. The matter was not finished yet. I felt observed. As a test, I thought in the direction of the black magician and immediately a poisonous substance came back at me. Wow, that happened fast! The black magician was apparently still quite disgruntled by my intervening.

I pushed it away, but it didn't work and I realized that we would have to face off. How should I do this? I would have to connect to forces that matched his. That could only be Christ, the world-I. So I asked Christ for support, tried to hold myself pure in heart and mind, waited till I felt touched by Christ and my aura filled with energy, then sent streams of love to the black magician. I overwhelmed him with benevolence and love!

I thought of him while I did this: *Why in the world are you doing this?. . . Because you are hoping for an increase in power?. . . You will get this increase in power . . . But do you know where this will lead?. . . In the end you will end up like this black substance and will be excluded from the cosmic path of development and will be discarded . . . Frozen as black dross for eternity . . . Until then perhaps you will feel well . . . But do you see this end clearly before your eyes?. . . The spirits you have allied with do not speak about this end! . . . They try to obfuscate this, although they know about it . . . They need you to produce the most possible black dross . . . This is only created if people create it as a free deed . . . But in the end, you turn into black dross yourself!*

In this way, I directed my thoughts in his direction, wrapping myself in benevolence and love. This went on until the evening. A real wrestling match took place. A different energy came back from him that no longer attacked me, but which I permeated with my energy and attempted to lift up.

After a while, I noticed that I was still vulnerable, specifically, in my auric backspace in the back of the heart. Slowly, it dawned on me what to do. I could take the spiritual space I always create meditatively by thinking and pull it into the region of my heart and in this way I could make the heart unassailable. I now experienced a kind of feather mantle around me. I had the impression I could spiritually walk everywhere without getting hurt, as long as I held myself in this inner state.

Finally, I noticed that no more energy was coming from the black magician. I wished him well and had the impression that this chapter was finished.

I didn't know how the black magician experienced the encounter. I assumed this kind of thing did not often happen to him. In any case, his deed was neutralized to some degree during the time of the referendum. I assumed the energy he emanated influenced Hamburg. He was probably in the background as a person but played a role energetically. Perhaps he was not incarnated but was working from the realm of the dead.

On Sunday, June 13, 2004, the day of the referendum, I visited the earth being on the playground again. It seemed to be doing quite well, and to my surprise, wore a feather cloak.

Sunday was a day of waiting. Everything was running smoothly. The weather was friendly and inviting. We were concerned about the turnout at the polls being high enough to overcome the 20 percent consent clause. It was tight, but in the end it all fitted together perfectly. We rejoiced and celebrated. The CDU politicians were crushed and did not understand the world anymore.

Summary

For me, the week before the referendum was filled with spiritual experiences of an extraordinary density and intensity. Like a gift from heaven. I did my utmost to solve the tasks at hand in a quick-witted way. After these experiences, I found that it increasingly did not make sense to take on political actions without including the spiritual dimensions, and especially clear was the importance of caring for the elemental world. That is the human assignment of the future!

In sum, all the important levels came together:

- Christ, and the dead who are connected to him, form the spiritual universe, the context in which everything takes place.
- The light and impersonal angelic world permeates everything. The angels wait for humans to call them before they put their energies at our disposal.
- The avid and faithful helpers of the multifarious elemental world are concerned with detailed work. They need help from us humans.
- The etheric world is managed by the angels and elemental beings and receives its imprint from the planets.
- The adversarial forces, if not redeemed through human love and, instead, densified through conscious human deed, become impermeable black dross.
- Our responsibility as humans is for the future of earth evolution, with two poles of possible development: spiritual-ization (social sculpture) or becoming goo (incorrigible moon).
- The social processes in the human world are influenced by all these spheres.
- Today's intellectual consciousness knows nothing of all this.
- The human heart knows everything deep inside.

Naturally, I ask myself if the actions I have described really contributed to the success of the referendum. You cannot measure this, of course; just as you can't measure the effect of a single piece of advertising.

The day after the referendum, I returned once more to the Pan in Wohlers Park and leaned on the majestic tree that was its focal point. I felt into the Pan, opened my heart, brought myself to a meditative state, heartily thanked the elemental beings for the good cooperative work, and asked Pan to share my thanks with all of the elemental beings in Hamburg.

I stayed like this for a time. Suddenly, I noticed that the Pan had indeed shared my thanks and had taken me along while doing so. Inwardly, I spread myself over the tree and plant world of a large part of Hamburg. The Pan consisted of spiritual pathways streaming in all directions, guiding and regulating everything. Joyfully, I pulled myself together again and knew this attempt to actively cooperate with the angelic and elemental world was complete.

~⟨∘⟩~

Looking back now on my experiences in Hamburg, I notice the following: The giant of Lubenicke made it clear to me that the future of the nature elementals depends on how we humans develop. If the adversarial elementals produced by humans gain the upper hand, the nature elementals fall into ruin. This theme was already present in Hamburg, with the blocked earth being on the playground and the black dross; however, the dramatic dimension of what this means only now became clear to me.

These are my experiences with the elemental beings so far. What have others experienced and found out? I light the gas lantern and take a box of books out of the tent. This is part of my book collection on the elemental beings theme that I packed to bring with me on my trip.

∽ 19 ∾

What the Elemental Being
Research Says

Communication is vital in spiritual research, just as it is in any other science. The quality of the research depends on comparing and sharing experiences. I am always curious to know what others have experienced with elemental beings and what connections they have found. Who has done research about elemental beings? What do others say about the relationship between humans and elemental beings? I spread the books in front of me.

The books by Vera Stael von Holstein pile up to a considerable height. Vera is a former computer programmer, lives in an old mill, and has practiced contacting the elementals since childhood. Since 2000, she has documented her conversations with the elementals in her mill. These elementals have been trained in human communication, so Vera can interview them in a highly differentiated way. Her books are a treasure trove for research on the elementals. Her elemental beings are fond of communication. There are presently several working groups that deal with medical, therapeutic, and agricultural questions by consulting the elementals of the mill.

Regarding the relationship between humans and elemental beings, Vera Stael von Holstein says:

> Without nature beings we could not exist. The whole earth
> would fall apart without their work. They are always involved
> in the growth and decay processes in nature—in the smallest
> plant as well as the overall climate. Nature beings are bound to
> wisdom-filled nature at large. And for them to be able to work

in this wise way, an angelic being or higher being always guides them from above. They work on behalf of this higher wisdom.

Today, however, the responsibility of the angels is gradually being placed on us humans. Human beings are responsible for nature. They have to concern themselves with the earth and with nature. They are responsible for their own ideas, feelings, and deeds, with which they constantly create new beings. But humans can only live up to their responsibility if they cooperate with nature spirits, if they know about them and their tasks. And nature spirits need this cooperation in order to be able to fulfill their tasks with regard to the wellbeing of the earth and of humanity.

You can compare the present situation of the nature spirits with the work of a business that no longer has a responsible CEO. Because the new boss has no consciousness of his responsibility, it becomes harder and harder for the nature spirits to fulfill their tasks. They were created to be led. Nature spirits want to know if what they are doing is right. They want to know if their creativity is still capable of keeping the world going. The nature spirits come and ask, "Am I doing it right, boss?" But the boss does not even know about their existence.[4]

Rudolf Steiner, the founder of anthroposophy, was a pioneer of spiritual research. In the 354 volumes of his collected works, you can find distinct descriptions of all the regions of the supersensible worlds. It was Steiner's intention to put in place foundations of spiritual research so that these could unfold as a cultural impulse with the depth and precision of natural science. Steiner attained a high degree of clairvoyance and was philosophically and scientifically trained. He was at great pains to unite the descriptions of his supersensible research with the precision of natural science. He made comments about elemental beings throughout his work.

---

[4] The quote is from "Was die Naturgeister uns sagen", *Flensburger Hefte 79*. Flensburg: Flensburger Hefte Verlag, 2002, S. 35 ff.

His 354 books add up to a lot of weight, so I have the collected works of Steiner on a hard disk, which I can carry anywhere in my briefcase. I now open the collected works and look for some important passages about the relationship of human being to elemental being.

In the lecture of April 12, 1909 in Düsseldorf (GA 110), Rudolf Steiner speaks of the enchantment and redemption of elemental beings. Briefly summarized, he comes to the following astonishing conclusions:

Matter is created by higher angelic hierarchies enchanting elemental beings into fire, air, water, and earth. Through wisdom-filled, empathetic, inner penetration of their sense perceptions, human beings can redeem these elemental beings from their enchantment, but if we stare dully and uncomprehendingly at the world, human beings leave these elementals in their enchantment. Redeemed elemental beings can stay in this state after the human being has died, whereas, unredeemed elementals must appear again with the human being in their enchantment.

The seasons come about through elemental beings of the summer being chained in the winter. Through a religious experience of the seasons, human beings redeem elemental beings from their winter enchantment. Through godlessness, human beings leave the elemental beings in their enchantment. Redeemed elemental beings can, after the death of the human being, stay in their summer state; unredeemed elemental beings must, however, reappear with the human being in their chained state.

The redemption of elemental beings happens through wise, inner, heartfelt sense experience, through a creative, diligent, productive life and through religious experience of the seasons according to Steiner.

In the lecture of May 28, 1922 in Dornach (GA 212), Steiner puts into words the worry of the giants of Lubenicke exactly. If we humans do not come to an experience and a concrete knowledge of spiritual beings in the world, the elemental beings of the earth, the water, and the air will succumb to Ahriman and the elemental beings of the light and the ether to Lucifer. Through this, the future of the earth would be endangered.

On September 28, 1923 in Vienna (GA 233), Rudolf Steiner describes how the nature elemental beings always flow into the human being and expect to be redeemed by them. Humans can do this if they build an emotional bond with the elementals. The adversarial forces, the dragons living inside the human being, also thirst after the elemental beings. If the human being leaves the elementals to the dragons, the earth will fall into decadence. Spiritually, this expresses itself today in materialistic thinking, on a soul level through cowardice, and on a physical level through bacteria. These are clear words!

Rudolf Steiner also dealt at great length with human-created elementals and the possibilities of the adversarial forces to inform these. His descriptions make the concerns of the giant of Lubenicke even more understandable.

Our auric emanations attract corresponding elemental beings that influence and shape our lives (see GA 194, Dornach, December 6, 1919).

Through the free weaving together of human feelings in human communities, high group souls are attracted emanating freedom. If the human being stays isolated, he develops into an evil elemental being (see GA 102, Berlin, June 1, 1908).

We humans create the following adversarial elementals: Phantoms through lies and slander (hardening of the physical body), ghosts through bad laws and discord in the social life (hardening of the ether body), and demons through overpowering others (hardening of the astral body). After death, these bad elementals disperse and populate the world (see GA 102, Berlin, June 4, 1908).

In my box, I have many more books by clairvoyant people who can communicate with elemental beings. These authentic reports are all moving and instructive. I have to admit that evaluating and comparing this research material would be its own huge project. I cannot do this; tomorrow our time in Valun is up. In order to do it properly, I would have to write another book. This would also be a good theme for a dissertation. Perhaps someday, someone will have the idea to write such a dissertation.

While packing, I flip through the pages of a book by Daphne Charters and find the following beautiful sentences: "The main work of the elves is to gather strength, to coarsen it enough to be used on Earth and then to breathe this strength into the astral bodies of their charges . . . . If human beings have the wish to give someone else strength, be it to heal, to comfort, or to love, they open up and the strength flows through them" (p. 23). "For the elves this strength is work, sustenance, drink, recuperation, and making love all at once, and their whole life consists of the gathering and giving of strength in different forms" (p. 47).[5]

---

[5] Daphne Charters. *Naturgeister und Menschen*. Grafing: Aquamarin Verlag, 2001. Originally published in 1956.

⁓ **20** ⁓

Departure

Our vacation in Valun is over today, and we pack everything up. I have the first version of *Answering the Call of the Elementals* in my bag. I glanced through it after breakfast and could feel how far removed it is from the "normal world." What effect will it have? Will it inspire people? Will inner deeds follow? Will it contribute to tipping the scales of world karma in the other direction? Will the elemental beings be freed of their concerns? Will their hopes be fulfilled?

On the ferry, I look back on Cres and the last weeks. A thunder storm rolls up. The island suddenly disappears. I see only fog and rain, and the strong wind pricks like needles on my face. Cres is gone! Disappeared into the fog just like that!

Yes, this intense time is over. I notice a strong pull in my heart and an inner wistfulness. The elemental beings of Cres have grown close to my heart.

Lara the light fairy comes along. This morning I asked the dwarf of Beley at the harbor wall what his plans were. He wants to come along and is looking forward to future experiences. The others will perhaps visit if I think of them.

Epilogue

M y vision for the future includes elemental beings once again becoming a cultural public resource for our civilization. I think of it in the following way.

In school, alongside mathematics and biology, there is a subject called Study of Elemental Beings. In local government, there is a department devoted to Care of Elemental Beings to help blocked elemental beings and represent the desires of elemental beings in other communal departments and for the public at large. It becomes commonplace to speak to the elementals before important decisions, just as you seek the advice of human experts. Little elementals become popular birthday presents that one focuses on a stone or other object.

At universities, there are several chairs concerning themselves with elemental research. Every year, hundreds of dissertations, diploma theses, and college papers get published. In different vocations, co-creation of elemental beings is taken into consideration. Doctors and healing practitioners communicate with the body elementals of their patients when diagnosing and prescribing therapies. Pastoral workers and psychologists deal with resolving the negative elementals that the patient has themself created through problematic belief systems and habits.

It is expected of cleaning companies that they clean buildings with the help of the local elemental beings. It is expected of farmers that strong and shiny elemental beings populate their fields and arable lands. It is expected of workers that they have a good connection to the elementals of their machines. Electronic control of machines is gradually replaced by direct meditative communication with the machine elementals. It is expected of managers that they have an eye on the elementals and angels living in the soul–spiritual space of their business community. Just as there are labels ensuring good organic quality today, there will be labels ensuring good treatment of elemental beings.

This vision is surely unfamiliar today and beyond the normal conceptual frame. To me, it is not only realistic but necessary. The nature elementals are eagerly waiting for human beings to consciously grasp them, for their future existence is dependent on it. We humans and the elemental beings have a common destiny—to rescue the elemental beings.

The question concerning the elementals touches on two very deep themes:

1 *The question of the connection between the human being and the world:* Do we feel connected to the world, at home in it, and responsible for it? Or do we feel disconnected, homeless, and not responsible for the world?

2 *The question of our self-understanding as human beings:* Are we spiritually free beings who experience and care for the flock of elementals composing our own personalities? Or are we driven by impulses and sentiments we cannot see eye to eye with?

You cannot answer these questions theoretically, only practically, and only if you start on the path of experiencing elemental beings. The next two books, *Collaboration with the Elemental Beings,* will offer further help for those on this path and will contain many conversations with people who have a conscious connection to elemental beings in which I ask them how they do it.

I wish you much luck and joy with this. Do something with it, and don't forget: Your elemental friends are always around and inside you!

Bibliography

Aderhold, Hans-Joachim and Thomas Mayer, (Hrsg.). *Erlebnis Erdwandlung – Berichte und Texte einer Zeitzeugenschaft.* Borchen: Möllmann Verlag, 2008.

Bachmann, Fritz. *Getragen von Engeln und Elementarwesen, Die ätherischen Hüllen des Goetheanums.* Schaffhausen: Oratio Verlag, 2003.

Bäzner, Erhard. *Die Naturgeister, Aus dem Reich der Gnomen, Nixen, Sylphen, Salamander und Sturmgeister.* Grafing: Aqamarin Verlag, 2007. Originally published in 1924.

Beusch, Christine. *Uns gibt es wirklich, Leben mit Elementarwesen.* Dornach: Pforte Verlag, 2010.

Bloom, William. *Working with Angels, Fairies and Nature Spirits.* London: Piatkus Books, 2010.

Burkhard, Ursula. *Karlik: Encounters with Elemental Beings.* Edinburgh, Scotland: Floris Books, 2017.

Cerny, Christine. *Das Buch der Naturgeister. Von Elfen, Zwergen, Feen und anderen Elementarwesen.* München: Goldmann Verlag, 2004.

Chales-de Beaulieu, Berthold. *Meine Gartengeister, Gespräche mit Naturwesen.* Regensburg: RiWei-Verlag, 2005.

Charters, Daphne. *Naturgeister und Menschen.* Grafing: Aquamarin Verlag, 2001. Originally published in 1956.

Crombie, R. Ogilvie. *Encounters with Nature Spirits: Co-creating with the Elemental Kingdom.* 3rd edition. Forres, Scotland: Findhorn Press, 2018.

Daskalos, Dr. Stylianos Atteshlis. *Die Esoterische Praxis.* Duisburg: EDEL Druck Verlag, 1996.

Grünn, Anna Cecilia. *Ellenlang: Meine Reise mit den Naturgeistern durch Deutschland.* Flensburg: Flensburger Hefte Verlag, 2009.

Helliwell, Tanis. *Pilgrimage with the Leprechauns.* Canada: Wayshower Enterprises, 2012.

———. *Summer with the Leprechauns.* Powell River, Canada: Tanis Helliwell Corporation, 2011.

Johnson, Marjorie. *Naturgeister, Wahre Erlebnisse mit Elfen und Zwerge.* Grafing: Aquamarin Verlag, 2000. Originally published in 1957.

Krauss, Ernst-Martin. *Holzwege, Steinwege . . . : Erlebnisse mit Elementarwesen.* Flensburg: Flensburger Hefte Verlag, 1992.

Kriele, Alexa. *Naturgeister erzählen.* Seeon: Ch. Falk Verlag, 1999.

———. *Von Naturgeistern lernen, Die Botschaften von Elfen, Feen und anderen guten Geistern.* München: Heinrich Hugendubel Verlag, 2005.

Kruse, Dirk. *Seelisches Beobachten in der Natur.* Groß Heins: Selbstverlag, 2003.

Lechner-Knecht, Sigrid. *Die Hüter der Elemente, Das geheimnisvolle Reich der Naturgeister.* Berlin: Zerling, 1993.

Massei, Karsten. *School of the Elemental Beings.* Hudson, NY: SteinerBooks, 2017.

Mayer, Thomas. *Zusammenarbeit mit Elementarwesen – 13 Gespräche mit Praktikern.* Saarbrücken: Neue Erde Verlag, 2010.

Mayer, Thomas. *Zusammenarbeit mit Elementarwesen 2 – Neue Interviews mit Forschern und Praktikern.* Saarbrücken: Neue Erde Verlag, 2012.

Pogacik, Marko. *Nature Spirits & Elemental Beings: Working with the Intelligence in Nature.* Forres, Scotland: Findhorn Press 2010.

Raven, Susan. *Nature Spirits: The Remembrance: A Guide to the Elemental Kingdom.* West Hoathly, UK: Clairview Books, 2013.

Rendtorff, Ilse. *Mit Wünschelruten Kraftorte und Naturwesen entdecken.* Saarbrücken: Verlag Neue Erde, 2002.

———. *Naturmeditationen: Heilung für Mensch und Erde. Von den ersten Schritten bis zur tiefen Erfahrung.* Saarbrücken: Verlag Neue Erde, 1999.

Ripley, Frances. *Visions Unseen, Aspects of the Natural Realm.* Findhorn Press, 2007.

Roessner, Ralf. *The Genius of Bees and the Elemental Beings.* Hudson, NY: Steiner Books, 2017.

Schweizer, Evelyn. *Unsere guten Nachbarn, Elfen, Gnomen und andere Naturwesen in der Schweiz.* Bern: Zytglogge Verlag, 2007.

Stecher, Christine. *Das kleine Buch der Feen und Elfen.* München: Mosaik Verlag, 2000.

Stefánsdóttir, Erla. *Lífssýn min, Lebenseinsichten der isländischen Elfenbeauftragten.* Saarbrücken: Verlag Neue Erde, 2007.

Steiner, Rudolf. *Our Connection with the Elemental World: 7 Lectures by Rudolf Steiner.* Forest Row, UK: Rudolf Steiner Press, 2017.

———. *Nature Spirits, Selected Lectures by Rudolf Steiner.* Forest Row, UK: Rudolf Steiner Press, 2016.

———. *Ernst Hagemann, Weltenäther – Elementarwesen – Naturreiche: Texte aus der Geisteswissenschaft Rudolf Steiners.* Oratio Verlag, 2001.

Van Gelder, Dora. *The Real World of Fairies: A First-Person Account*, 2nd edition. Wheaton, IL: Quest Books, 1999.

Von Holstein, Verena Stael. *Was die Naturgeister uns sagen, Naturgeister 1, Im Interview direkt befragt.* Flensburg: Flensburger Hefte Verlag, 2002.

———. *Neue Gespräche mit den Naturgeistern, Naturgeister 2.* Flensburg: Flensburger Hefte Verlag, 2002.

Weirauch, Wolfgang. *Nature Spirits of the Trees and What They Want to Tell Us: Messages from the Beings of the Trees.* West Hoathly, UK: Clairview Books, 2020.

———. *Nature Spirits and What They Say: Interviews with Verena Holstein.* Edinburgh, Scotland: Floris Books, 2005.

Wright, Machaelle Small. *MAP: Medical Assistance Program.* Warrenton, VA: Perelandra Ltd., 1990.

About the Author

Photo by Christian Flemming

Thomas Mayer is an author, civil rights activist, and meditation teacher. He was born in 1965 in Kempten, Allgäu, in Austria and is co-founder of More Democracy, an association concerned with participatory politics. He was the authorized representative of the successful referendum More Democracy in Bavaria from 1993 to 1995. Until 2006, Thomas was on the board of the Omnibus for Direct Democracy as councilor for regional currencies, and from 2013 to 2018, he was campaign manager for the Swiss positive money initiative. Since 2005, he has worked primarily as a teacher of anthroposophic meditation. Thomas teaches throughout Europe and lives near Basel, Switzerland.

For more information see **www.thomasmayer.org** and **www.anthroposophische-meditation.de**.

FINDHORN PRESS

Life-Changing Books

Learn more about us and our books at
www.findhornpress.com

For information on the Findhorn Foundation:
www.findhorn.org